BST

ID0780394

HOW TO CHANGE YOUR NAME

by
Margaret C. Jasper

Oceana's Legal Almanac Series:
Law for the Layperson

2005
Oceana Publications, Inc.
Dobbs Ferry, New York

You may order this or any Oceana publication by visiting Oceana's website at http://www.oceanalaw.com

Library of Congress Control Number: 2005925303

ISBN 0-379-11393-7

Oceana's Legal Almanac Series: Law for the Layperson
ISSN 1075-7376

Manufactured in the United States of America on acid-free paper.

To My Husband Chris

Your love and support
are my motivation and inspiration

-and-

In memory of my son, Jimmy

Table of Contents

ABOUT THE AUTHOR

MARGARET C. JASPER is an attorney engaged in the general practice of law in South Salem, New York, concentrating in the areas of personal injury and entertainment law. Ms. Jasper holds a Juris Doctor degree from Pace University School of Law, White Plains, New York, is a member of the New York and Connecticut bars, and is certified to practice before the United States District Courts for the Southern and Eastern Districts of New York, the United States Court of Appeals for the Second Circuit, and the United States Supreme Court.

Ms. Jasper has been appointed to the panel of arbitrators of the American Arbitration Association and the law guardian panel for the Family Court of the State of New York, is a member of the Association of Trial Lawyers of America, and is a New York State licensed real estate broker and member of the Westchester County Board of Realtors, operating as Jasper Real Estate, in South Salem, New York. Margaret Jasper maintains a website at http://www.JasperLawOffice.com.

Ms. Jasper is the author and general editor of the following legal almanacs: AIDS Law; The Americans with Disabilities Act; Animal Rights Law; The Law of Attachment and Garnishment; Bankruptcy Law for the Individual Debtor; Individual Bankruptcy and Restructuring; Banks and their Customers; Buying and Selling Your Home; The Law of Buying and Selling; The Law of Capital Punishment; The Law of Child Custody; Your Rights in a Class Action Suit; Commercial Law; Consumer Rights Law; The Law of Contracts; Copyright Law; Credit Cards and the Law; The Law of Debt Collection; Dictionary of Selected Legal Terms; The Law of Dispute Resolution; Drunk Driving Law; DWI, DUI and the Law; Education Law; Elder Law; Employee Rights in the Workplace; Employment Discrimination Under Title VII; Environmental Law; Estate Planning; Everyday Legal Forms; Executors and Personal Representatives: Rights and Responsibilities; Harassment in the Workplace; Health Care and Your Rights. Home Mortgage Law Primer; Hospital Liability Law; Identity Theft and How To Protect Yourself; Insurance Law; The Law of Immigration; International Adoption; Juvenile Justice and Children's Law; Labor Law; Landlord-Tenant Law; The Law of Libel and Slander; Living Together: Practical Legal Issues; Marriage and Divorce; The Law of Medical Malpractice; Motor Vehicle Law; The Law of No-Fault Insurance; Nursing Home Negligence; The Law of Obscenity and Pornography; Patent Law; The Law of Personal Injury; The Law of Premises Liability; Prescription Drugs; Privacy and the Internet: Your Rights and Expectations Under the Law; Probate Law; The Law of Product Liability; Real Estate Law for the Homeowner and Broker; Religion and the Law; Retirement Planning; The Right to Die; Rights of Single Parents; Law for the Small Business Owner; Small Claims Court; Social Security Law; Special Education Law; The Law of Speech and the First Amendment; Teenagers and Substance Abuse; Trademark Law; Victim's Rights Law; The Law of Violence Against Women; Welfare: Your Rights and the Law; What if it Happened to You: Violent Crimes and Victims' Rights; What if the Product Doesn't Work: Warranties & Guarantees; Workers' Compensation Law; and Your Child's Legal Rights: An Overview.

INTRODUCTION

For most of your life, your name has been your identity, and inevitably you have formed an emotional attachment to your name. Therefore, deciding to change your name can be a very difficult decision, regardless of your reasons for doing so. Legally, you are allowed to change your name to any name you choose. You can change your first name, last name, or both. The only exception is that you cannot change your name for an illegal or fraudulent purpose, as further discussed in this almanac.

This almanac discusses the practical and legal aspects of changing one's name, and the procedure one must follow in order for the name change to have legal effect. Notification is also an important part of implementing your name change. After all, what sense does it make to change your name if you don't tell anyone to use your new name.

The almanac provides a list of important government agencies and private institutions that you should contact after your name change is official, with instructions on how to go about requesting the name change. In addition, the types of documents which should be amended or replaced following a name change are also discussed.

The Appendix provides applicable statutes, sample forms, and other pertinent information and data. The Glossary contains definitions of many of the terms used throughout the almanac.

CHAPTER 1:
CHANGING YOUR NAME

YOUR NAME AND YOUR IDENTITY

"A rose by any other name would smell as sweet"—William Shakespeare

Your name is your identity, and although changing your name does not change who you are inside, it can be a very difficult and personal decision. After all, your name is the one word that makes you turn your head in a crowd when you hear it called. It is one of the first words you respond to as an infant. It is usually the word you answered to throughout your childhood. Your parents, your siblings, your friends, teachers, coaches, co-workers all knew you "by your name." Your academic achievements, diplomas, awards all have your name imprinted on them. In fact, for many, the legal process of changing one's name is much easier than the emotional process.

NAME DEFINED

Although there may be variations in the definition of "name" among the states, Maryland's statutory definition of "name" is typical, as follows:

Annotated Code of Maryland—Transportation Article § 11-137

"Name" means:

(1) True or legal name;

(2) In the case of an individual, the name given at birth to the individual by his parents, or as changed under the common law of this State or any other state, by marriage, or by court order; and

(3) In the case of an individual party to an absolute divorce, the individual may elect to use any legal or true name previously used by the individual if this name is used consistently and nonfraudulently.

REASONS FOR CHANGING YOUR NAME

As the Maryland statute indicates, two common reasons people change their name are marriage and divorce. However, there are a number of other reasons a person may want to change their name. Some people change their name for religious reasons. Others want to change their name because they simply do not like their birth name, or because they have been adopted.

In some cases, an individual may want to change their name to avoid embarrassment because some infamous criminal has sensationalized the name. An entertainer may want to assume a stage name. On a serious note, many people have to change their name if they are being harassed or if they are trying to escape from an abusive relationship and do not want to be easily located.

Often due to language barriers, many immigrants who came to this country through ports of entry, such as Ellis Island, had their names misspelled or shortened by immigration officials. Sometimes their surname was completely overlooked, and was mistakenly recorded as the place from which they emigrated. In those cases, their descendants may want to reclaim their original family name.

LIMITATIONS ON CHANGING YOUR NAME

Generally, you can pick any name you choose, for yourself or your minor child, with some exceptions, as discussed below.

Fraud or Illegality

As the Maryland statute indicates, you cannot change your name for fraudulent purposes. For example, you cannot assume a new name as part of an illegal scheme to defraud others, or to avoid prosecution for a criminal act. Further, you cannot legally change your name to avoid paying debts, shield yourself from a lawsuit, or elude law enforcement or immigration officials.

Many states have statutory provisions that prohibit convicted sex offenders from changing their name. Idaho's statute contains such a provision, as follows:

IDAHO CODE §7-805—RESTRICTIONS ON NAME CHANGES FOR CONVICTED SEXUAL OFFENDERS—NOTIFICATION OF NAME CHANGES OF CONVICTED SEXUAL OFFENDERS

(1) No person shall apply for a change of name with the intent or purpose of avoiding registration as a convicted sexual offender pursuant to chapter 83, title 18, Idaho Code. No name change shall be granted to any person if the name change would have the effect of relieving the person of the duty to register as a convicted sexual offender under chapter 83, title 18, Idaho Code, or under the provisions of similar laws enacted by another state.

(2) The court granting a name change to any individual required to register as a convicted sexual offender pursuant to the provisions of chapter 83, title 18, Idaho Code, shall provide notice of the name change to the Idaho department of law enforcement, central sexual offender registry. This notice shall include the offender's name prior to change, new name, social security number, date of birth and last known address.

Selective Service Registration

If you are between the ages of 18 and 26, you must be registered with the Selective Service System. If you change your name, you must notify Selective Service so that they can amend their records. You cannot change your name as a means of avoiding registration. Changing your name with the Selective Service System is discussed more fully in Chapter 5 of this almanac.

Interference with the Rights of Others

You cannot choose a name that would interfere with the rights of others. For example, you cannot use the name of a famous person if you are doing so for fraudulent purposes or financial benefit. If you are considering renaming yourself Donald Trump, you better have a good reason for choosing such a well-recognized name, or the judge will likely deny your petition. In addition, you generally cannot use a fictitious name that has been copyrighted.

Confusing Names

You cannot use a name that would be intentionally confusing, such as a number or a punctuation mark.

Fighting Words

You cannot use a name that would be considered a "fighting word," such as an obscenity or racial slur.

Thus, before a court will consider your request for a name change, you will usually be required to state whether any of the following situations apply to you:

1. You have been convicted of a crime.

2. You have filed for and been granted bankruptcy relief.

3. You are presently the defendant in a lawsuit.

4. You are presently in the middle of a divorce action.

5. You are between the ages of 18 and 26.

6. You are a legal resident alien, a naturalized citizen or a non-resident alien.

ADDITIONAL NAME CHANGES

In some states, you are not allowed to change your name more than one time without just cause, unless the change is connected with marriage or divorce. Iowa's name change statute contains such a provision, as follows:

Iowa Code § 674.13 Further change barred.

A person shall not change the person's name more than once under this chapter unless just cause is shown. However, in a decree dissolving a person's marriage, the person's name may be changed back to the name appearing on the person's original birth certificate or to a legal name previously acquired in a former marriage.

CHAPTER 2:
NAME CHANGE PROCEDURE

IN GENERAL

Although changing your name does not involve a difficult or complicated procedure, it used to be much easier. For example, before identity theft and terrorism raised concerns, you could simply pick a new name, openly and consistently start using it in your business and social affairs, and eventually the new name would stick, and become your legal name. It was not necessary to file any papers in court. This name change procedure is known as "common usage." Now it is preferable to obtain a court order.

COMMON USAGE

As set forth above, in those states that still adhere to the common usage doctrine for a legal name change, you do not need a court order and you can still legally change your name by simply adopting a new name, using it and insisting that others use it as well.

Although most states still allow individuals to legally change their name through common usage, most government agencies and private businesses are not comfortable with such an informal way of changing one's name. Therefore, it is unlikely that any government agency or private institution, such as a bank, will amend their official records to reflect your new name without a court order. In fact, certain documents, such as a passport, birth certificate and social security card cannot be amended without a court order, with few exceptions, e.g. a marriage license.

If you are adamant about avoiding a formal court procedure, you can try to enforce the law by providing a copy of the state law that supports your position. If you are stonewalled, then go up the chain of command until you find someone who will listen to you. However, it is likely that you will run into a lot of opposition when trying to change your name in this manner, even if it is the law.

Thus, even if name changes under the common usage method are legal in your state, it is better to get a court order allowing you to officially start using your new name. You can determine whether or not a court order is required in your state in order to legally change your name by checking your state's name change statute.

A directory of state name change laws is set forth at Appendix 1.

FILING THE NAME CHANGE PETITION

A name change petition is a form that you fill out which basically asks the judge for permission to change your name, and sets forth your reasons for wanting the name change. The petition is usually required to be signed before, and witnessed by, a notary public. The clerk of the court may be a notary. In addition, many bank officers are also notaries.

A sample adult name change petition is set forth at Appendix 2.

In addition to the name change petition, depending on the state, there are other documents which must be filed with the Court, along with the appropriate filing fee, in order to initiate a name change proceeding. Typically, the required forms include:

1. A petition for name change;

2. A notice for publication;

3. An order for name change;

4. All necessary attachments—e.g., proof of identity, etc.

You can check with your local court clerk to find out whether there are any additional forms which need to be filed. Many state courts now have websites from which official forms can be downloaded to your computer.

A sample adult name change packet with instructions is set forth at Appendix 3.

Name change kits are also available over the internet, which take you step-by-step through the name change process and provide all of the forms necessary to change your name in your state.

PROOF OF IDENTITY

Along with the petition, you will generally be required to prove your identity before the name change order can be signed. A birth certificate will suffice as proof of identity if you are a U.S. citizen who was born in the United States. If you are a naturalized U.S. citizen, you must provide a copy of your naturalization papers, and if you are a permanent resident alien, you must provide a copy of your alien registration card—commonly referred to as a "green card."

PUBLICATION REQUIREMENT

Most states require you to publish an announcement in the local newspaper in order to give the public notice of your proposed name change. The judge may instruct you as to the newspaper in which you must publish the announcement. You will have to pay a fee to the newspaper for this service. The newspaper will provide you with an "affidavit of publication," which must be filed with the court within a certain time period after publication.

California's statute is typical of the publication requirement, as follows:

California Code § 1276 Civ. Proc.

. . .[W]here an action for a change of name is commenced by the filing of a petition, the court shall thereupon make an order reciting the filing of the petition, the name of the person by whom it is filed and the name proposed, and directing all persons interested in the matter to appear before the court at a time and place specified, which shall be not less than four or more than eight weeks from the time of making the order, to show cause why the application for change of name should not be granted. A copy of the order to show cause shall be published pursuant to Section 6064 of the Government Code in a newspaper of general circulation to be designated in the order published in the county. If no newspaper of general circulation is published in the county, a copy of the order to show cause shall be posted by the clerk of the court in three of the most public places in the county in which the court is located, for a like period. Proof shall be made to the satisfaction of the court of this publication or posting, at the time of the hearing of the application. Four weekly publications shall be sufficient publication of the order to show cause. If the order is published in a daily newspaper, publication once a week for four successive weeks shall be sufficient. . .]

Exemption from Publication Requirement

In the case of a person who is escaping an abusive situation, he or she may request an exemption from the publication requirement in order to protect their identity and safety. This makes sense since requiring publication in such a case would defeat the purpose for the name change in the first place.

Colorado's name change statute addresses this situation, as follows:

Colorado Code §13-15-102 - Publication of change.

(2) Public notice of such name change through publication as required in subsection (1) of this section shall not be required if the petitioner has been:

(a) The victim of a crime, the underlying factual basis of which has been found by the court on the record to include an act of domestic violence, as defined in section 18-6-800.3 (1), C.R.S.;

(b) The victim of child abuse, as defined in section 18-6-401, C.R.S.; or

(c) The victim of domestic abuse as that term is defined in section 14-4-101 (2), C.R.S.

COURT APPEARANCE

Once your name change petition is filed, some states require a court appearance before a judge, who will review your petition and supporting documentation, and ask any relevant questions. After reviewing your petition, the judge will decide whether or not to grant your name change request. If the petition is approved, the judge will sign a court order permitting you to use the new name, and return a signed copy to you. In some states, the judge signs the name change order based solely on the documents submitted.

LEGAL REPRESENTATION

If you don't feel comfortable filing your own name change petition and appearing in court before a judge, you can hire a lawyer to handle the process on your behalf. Some states allow paralegals, who are less expensive, to file name change petitions. In addition, as set forth above, there are online services that provide the state-specific forms necessary for changing your name on your own. Some of these services also employ a legal staff who will help you fill out the forms and/or handle the name change on your behalf. Two of these online services are: "namechangelaw.com" and "uslegalforms.com."

EXCEPTIONS TO COURT ORDER REQUIREMENT

In certain situations, a legal name change will be automatically recognized as a result of certain documents that may be issued and, therefore, there is no need to file a formal petition with the Court.

Marriage and Divorce

If you marry and change your name to your husband's surname following marriage, the marriage license serves as acceptable proof that your name has legally changed. Following divorce, if requested, your divorce decree may contain a provision changing your name back to your maiden name, and also serves as acceptable proof of your name change.

Name change following marriage or divorce is discussed more fully in Chapter 4 of this almanac.

Naturalization

An automatic name change can also occur when a legal alien becomes an American citizen. If you wish to change your name as part of your naturalization, you can do so provided a court in your area conducts the naturalization oath ceremonies. If not, your name change cannot be recorded on your Certificate of Naturalization unless your name has already been changed legally before the naturalization process has been completed.

Adoption

Adoption proceedings provide an opportunity to legally change a child's name. The child's new name is set forth in the adoption decree, which serves as acceptable proof of the child's new name. Wyoming's statute provides for name change following adoption, as follows:

Wyoming Statute §1-25-104. Change of name in adoption proceedings.

In all cases of the adoption of children in the manner provided by law, the court before which such adoption proceeding is held, may change the name of any child so adopted and make an order to that effect, which shall be recorded in the records of the proceeding of adoption. Each child who has heretofore, in Wyoming, been adopted according to law, may have his or her name changed to that of the parents who have adopted him or her, upon the parents, who have adopted such child, on behalf of such child, filing a petition therefor.

COSTS

The total cost of obtaining a name change is minimal. If you decide to purchase a name change kit, this will be your initial cost, and there may be a nominal fee for having your petition notarized. Generally, you will be required to pay a filing fee to the Court at the time you file your petition and supporting documents. You can check with your local court clerk to find out the applicable filing fee.

In addition to the filing fee, you will have to pay for the cost of publishing your name change announcement in the newspaper. You will also need to pay a small fee to obtain a copy of your amended birth certificate, and certified copies of the name change order.

CHAPTER 3:
CHANGING YOUR CHILD'S NAME

FILING THE NAME CHANGE PETITION

The procedure for obtaining a court order to change your minor child's name is pretty much the same as the steps set forth in Chapter 2 describing how an adult obtains a name change. However, the petition which needs to be filed is different for a child under the age of 18.

A sample child name change petition is set forth at Appendix 4.

In addition to the name change petition, depending on the state, there are other documents which must be filed with the Court, along with the appropriate filing fee, in order to initiate a name change proceeding. Typically, the required forms include:

1. A petition for name change;

2. A notice for publication;

3. An order for name change;

4. Consent form;

5. All necessary attachments—e.g., proof of identity, etc.

You can check with your local court clerk to find out whether there are any additional forms which need to be filed with a child name change petition. Many state courts now have websites from which official forms can be downloaded to your computer.

A sample child name change packet with instructions is set forth at Appendix 5.

Child name change kits are also available over the internet, which take you step-by-step through the name change process and provide all of the forms necessary to change your name in your state.

PROOF OF IDENTITY

In support of the child's name change petition, as with the adult petition, you will be required to provide proof of your child's identity before an order will be signed. Generally, a birth certificate will suffice as proof of identity for your child if he or she was born in the United States.

If your child is a naturalized U.S. citizen, you must provide a copy of their naturalization papers, and if your child is a permanent resident alien, you must provide a copy of their alien registration card—commonly referred to as a "green card."

Proof of the child's identity must be filed with the petition to change the child's name.

CONSENT

In addition to the above requirements, you will usually need to provide the Court with consent forms, depending on the situation. For example, if your child has reached a certain age, e.g., 14 or older, the Court will require the child to sign a consent form stating that they are requesting the name change.

Further, if the petition is filed by one parent, the Court will require the child's other parent to sign a consent form stating that they agree to the child's name change. In the case where a woman is trying to escape from an abusive relationship, and is in fear for her safety and the safety of her children, this situation must be brought to the Court's attention.

If you do not have a signed consent from the other parent because you do not know where her or she is, there are certain steps you must take in order to conduct a search and make a good faith attempt to notify the other parent before the name change order will be signed. All of the required consent forms must be filed with your petition for the name change.

Your reasons for requesting the name change must be significant. For example, if your spouse is adopting your child, you may want your child to have the same last name as your spouse. You may also want to change your child's name to match his or her stepparent, even if an adoption is not anticipated.

The consent provision of Iowa's name change statute is typical:

Iowa Code § 674.6 Notice—consent.

If the petitioner is married, the petitioner must give legal notice to the spouse, in the manner of an original notice, of the filing of the petition. If the petition includes or is filed on behalf of a minor child fourteen years of age or older, the child's written consent to the change of name of that child is required. If the petition includes or is filed on behalf of a minor child under fourteen, both parents as stated on the birth certificate of the minor child shall file their written consent to the name change. If one of the parents does not consent to the name change, a hearing shall be set on the petition on twenty days' notice to the non-consenting parent pursuant to the rules of civil procedure. At the hearing the court may waive the requirement of consent as to one of the parents if it finds:

1. That the parent has abandoned the child;

2. That the parent has been ordered to contribute to the support of the child or to financially aid in the child's birth and has failed to do so without good cause; or

3. That the parent does not object to the name change after having been given due and proper notice.

A sample consent form is set forth at Appendix 6.

REFUSAL TO CONSENT

If you know where the other parent is located, but he or she refuses to consent to the child's name change, you will generally be required to serve the petition and supporting documents on the other parent. If he or she contests the petition, you will have to argue the matter in a hearing before the Court, explaining why the child's name should be changed. The Court will use the "best interests of the child" standard in making his or her decision.

Nebraska's name change statute sets forth the criteria a Court considers in making a "best interests of the child" decision:

Nebraska Code § 61-101.

[W]hether a minor child's surname may be changed depends on, and is determined by, the best interests of the child. Factors to be considered are (1) the misconduct by one of the child's parents, (2) a parent's failure to support the child, (3) parental failure to maintain contact with the child, (4) the length of time that a surname has been used for or by the child, and (5) whether the child's surname is different from the surname of the child's custodial parent. Additionally, a court may consider the child's reasonable preference for a surname; the effect of the name change on the child's relationship with each parent; community respect associated with the surname; the difficulties, harassment, or embarrassment associated with either the present or proposed surname; and the identification of the child as part of the family unit.

PUBLICATION REQUIREMENT

The Court will generally require you to publish a notice about your child's name change petition in a newspaper of general circulation in the county in which the petition is filed. In some jurisdictions, the responsibility of publishing the notice is borne by the petitioner. In other jurisdictions, the clerk of the court is responsible for making publication arrangements. You should check with the clerk of the court to find out their procedure regarding publication.

After the notice has been published, interested parties are given the opportunity to object to the name change. If someone objects, they must file the objection with the Court and provide you with a copy. You are then given a certain amount of time to respond to the objection. After the Notice has been published, the newspaper will generally send confirmation of publication to you and to the Clerk of the Court.

THE NAME CHANGE ORDER

In many states, as long as the paperwork is in order, and nobody has objected to the name change, the Court will sign the Order. However, if there is an objection, or you were unable to obtain all of the necessary consents, or simply if the Court has any questions regarding the Petition, he or she will schedule a hearing. If the Court determines, following the hearing, that the name change is proper, the Court will sign the Order.

Once the Order is signed, you will receive a signed and certified copy of the Order. Additional certified copies can be obtained from the Clerk of the Court in which the petition was filed. The certified Order serves as proof of the child's name change, and should be filed with the appropriate parties, as set forth in Chapter 5 of this almanac.

RIGHTS AND OBLIGATIONS UNCHANGED

Merely changing your child's name does not mean that the child has been adopted. For example, just because you are successful in changing your child's name to that of your new spouse, this does not make the stepparent the legal parent of the child. Legal adoption is a more complicated procedure which must be formally brought before a Court.

In addition, changing a child's name does not relieve the biological parent from the responsibility of paying child support. For example, if your former spouse remarries and has your child's last name changed to match the stepparent, you are still required to pay child support for your child.

UNMARRIED PARENTS

In a marital relationship, the child generally takes the last name of the father and that is the name that appears on the child's birth certificate. Unmarried couples usually keep their own last names, thus, the question arises as to what last name should appear on the baby's birth certificate as his or her legal name.

There is no legal requirement that the child of a married or unmarried couple must take the last name of either parent. Thus, the child can have an entirely different last name if the parents so choose. However, this is rarely the case. Unmarried parents can use either the last name of the father or the mother, or they can choose to hyphenate both last names. If in the future the parents wish to amend the birth certificate—e.g., if they marry and want the child to use the father's last name—they can contact their state's bureau of vital statistics.

CHAPTER 4:
CHANGING YOUR NAME AFTER MARRIAGE OR DIVORCE

IN GENERAL

When you get married or divorced, changing your name is automatic. You do not have to go through the legal process described in Chapter 2. You can simply start using your new or old name, as the case may be. Although you will need to provide proof of your changed name, your marriage certificate or divorce decree will generally suffice.

Nevertheless, you are not obligated to change your name following marriage or divorce. New York's name change statute addresses this point, as follows:

New York State Consolidated Laws Article 6 §65. Optional change of name upon marriage, divorce or annulment.

1. Any person may, upon marriage, elect to assume a new name according to the provisions of paragraph (b) of subdivision one of section fifteen of the domestic relations law.

2. Any person may, upon divorce or annulment, elect to resume the use of a former surname according to the provisions of section 240a of the domestic relations law.

3. The effect of the name changes accomplished in the manner prescribed in subdivisions one and two of this section shall be as set forth in section sixty-four of this chapter.

4. Nothing in this article shall be construed to abrogate or alter the common law right of every person, whether married or single, to retain his or her name or to assume a new one so long as the new name is used consistently and without intent to defraud.

CHANGING YOUR NAME FOLLOWING MARRIAGE

If you are a woman, you probably took the surname of your husband when you got married. Although you can choose to continue using your maiden name, taking your husband's surname is traditionally the name change that takes place following a marriage. You should begin to use your new name after you are married. Properly notify all parties, and change your name on all of your documents, as set forth in Chapter 5 of this almanac. If you need to provide evidence of your new name, a certified copy of your marriage license will be sufficient proof.

Of course, there are many other less traditional choices you and your spouse can make. For example, you and your spouse can decide to hyphenate both of your surnames. You can both choose entirely new names. In fact, a husband can choose to take on his wife's surname. However, choosing a non-traditional name change will likely require a court order to implement.

There is an online service (www.kibitz.com) which offers a "new bride name change kit" that is state-specific and contains the required government forms, personal record change forms, instruction guides and a checklist to help the new bride change her name from her maiden name to her married name, including the following:

1. Social Security/IRS records

2. Drivers License

3. Vehicle Title/Registration

4. Voter Registration

5. U.S. Passport

6. Banking/Financial records

7. Vehicle Lease or Loan

8. Credit Cards

9. Insurance Records

10. Medical Records

11. Employment Records

This service also offers a "newlywed name change kit" for the bride and groom that want to change both of their names. This kit assists the bride and the groom in the application of using both the bride's family surname and the groom's family surname following marriage.

CHANGING YOUR NAME FOLLOWING DIVORCE

You can reclaim your maiden name following divorce provided you make this request as part of your divorce proceeding. The Court will include a provision in the divorce decree giving you the right to use your old name. If you need to provide evidence of your name change, a certified copy of your divorce decree will be sufficient proof.

However, as discussed above, if you want to continue to be known by your married name, you will not be forced to give up your ex-husband's surname even though you are no longer married. You simply continue to use the same name.

Maryland's name change statute contains a typical provision concerning name change following divorce, as follows:

Annotated Code of Maryland - Family Law Article § 7-105

In granting a decree of absolute divorce, the court shall change the name of a party to either the name given the party at birth or any other former name the party wishes to use if:

(1) the party took a new name on marriage and no longer wishes to use it;

(2) the party asks for the change of name; and

(3) the purpose of the party is not illegal, fraudulent, or immoral.

OBTAINING A NAME CHANGE AFTER THE DIVORCE DECREE IS ISSUED

If you did not request the right to reclaim your maiden name as part of the divorce proceeding, and you subsequently decide that you want to change your name, you will have to go back into Court and file a petition to change your name, as discussed in Chapter 2. Some states, however, allow you to go back into Court even after the divorce and make a request for restoration of your maiden name. Therefore, the reader is advised to check the law of his or her own jurisdiction in this regard.

In any event, if you still have evidence of your maiden name, such as your birth certificate, you can generally start using your maiden name again without a problem because you will still be able to prove your former identity in order to make changes to your records. If you do not have any evidence of your maiden name, you will likely have to petition the Court for an order so you can amend or replace documents that are still in your married name.

The online service referenced above (www.kibitz.com) also offers a "divorce name change kit." The kit contains the required government forms, personal record change forms, instruction guides and a checklist to assist a divorced woman seeking to reclaim her maiden name.

CHILDREN OF DIVORCE

Following a divorce, if you are the mother, you may decide that you want your child to bear your former maiden name, or the name of your new husband (stepfather) instead of the biological father's name. However, courts have traditionally ruled that you cannot unilaterally change the surnames of children following a divorce if the father continues in his parental role.

If you file a petition requesting the Court to change your child's name, the Court will make it's decision based on the best interests of the child. The Court will take into account certain factors, including but not limited to: (i) the relationship between the father and the child; (ii) the relationship between the mother and the child; (iii) the wishes of the child if the child is old enough to express his or her preference; and (iv) the length of time the child has been known by his or her name.

If you are successful in changing your child's surname, this does not constitute an adoption, change the identity of the child's father, and does not alter any parental rights or obligations, such as custody, visitation, child support, inheritance rights, etc. However, if the father's parental rights are terminated, or your child is adopted by his or her stepparent, with the consent of the child's father, the child's name can generally be changed as part of the adoption procedure.

WIDOWS AND WIDOWERS

An individual who becomes widowed is generally entitled to change their name back to their birth name. The North Carolina statute contains a typical provision concerning an application for a name change by a widow or widower, as follows:

North Carolina General Statutes 101-8. Resumption of name by widow or widower.

A person at any time after the person is widowed may, upon application to the clerk of court of the county in which the person resides setting forth the person's intention to do so, resume the use of her maiden name or the name of a prior deceased husband or of a previously divorced husband in the case of a widow, or his pre-marriage surname in the case of a widower. The application shall set forth the full name of the last spouse of the applicant, shall include a copy of the spouse's death certificate, and shall be signed by the applicant in the applicant's full name. The clerks of court of the several counties of this State shall record and index such applications in the manner required by the Administrative Office of the Courts.

CHAPTER 5:
USING YOUR NEW NAME

NOTIFYING OTHERS REGARDING YOUR NAME CHANGE

After your name change order has been signed, you can begin to use your new name. You should start using your new name consistently, and make sure that others are aware of this change. You should contact all government agencies and private businesses that you deal with and advise them that you have legally changed your name. Request all of your records to be updated and all future correspondence sent to you in care of your new name.

Don't forget to notify your friends and family and advise them of your name change. Ask them to start using your new name. Have your name officially changed at your place of employment and ask your co-workers to call you by your new name.

A checklist of places to contact following your name change is set forth at Appendix 7.

AMENDING AND REPLACING DOCUMENTS

In order to implement your new name, you should request an amendment to all of your official records and important documents. For example, if you have made any type of estate planning document, such as a will or trust, you should replace the document with a new document indicating your new name to avoid future confusion.

When contacting a government agency or private business, find out what is needed in order for your records to be amended. In some cases, a phone call will suffice. However, it is preferable, and more likely, that a letter will be required. There may be certain forms that need to be filled out, and certain documents they want you to produce. Many institutions will insist on proof of your new identity, therefore, you will have to include a copy of your court order.

Clearly show your old name and new name and explain that you want them to substitute your new name for your old name on all of their records. It helps to provide documents which show the transition between your old name and your new name. For example, a passport will have an "a/k/a" on it, demonstrating the previous and changed name.

The first items for which you should seek an amendment once your name is officially changed are your driver's license and social security card. Once you have been able to have your name changed on those documents, it will be much easier to have your name changed on other records. Most government agencies and private businesses accept these items as proof of one's identity.

It is important that you do not hastily discard any of your old documents. In fact, it is advisable to put documents and identification cards which contain your old name in a file and keep it in case you need to prove your previous identity for whatever reason.

A checklist of documents that should be replaced or amended following your name change is set forth at Appendix 8.

STATE DEPARTMENT OF VITAL RECORDS

In order to amend a birth certificate to reflect your new name, or the name of your minor child, you must contact your state bureau of vital records. Although state laws may vary, you will generally be required to produce the name change court order. Upon receipt of the court order, the birth certificate will be amended and you can obtain certified copies of the amended birth certificate. The state bureaus of vital records generally keeps a record of the original birth certificate and the date of the amendment.

A directory of state bureaus of vital records is set forth at Appendix 9.

STATE DEPARTMENT OF MOTOR VEHICLES

It is important to have your driver's license and automobile registration and title amended to reflect your new name. The forms you need are state-specific and are available at your local Department of Motor Vehicle (DMV) office. Some state DMV offices have websites from which you can download the necessary forms.

A directory of State Departments of Motor Vehicles is set forth at Appendix 10.

Driver's License

In order to change the name on your driver's license, most states require two forms of identification, e.g., the name change court order and your current driver's license. There are also other forms of identification the DMV will accept as proof of identity. Check with your local DMV office to find out which documents will suffice.

As an example, by statute, Maryland requires the following documentation in order to change the name on a driver's license:

Annotated Code of Maryland—Transportation Article § 16-106, 16-116 (Name on driver's license)

(e)(2) An individual party to an absolute divorce may elect to use a prior legal or true name upon filing an affidavit or other proof, satisfactory to the Administration, of:

(i) The prior name; and

(ii) The absolute divorce.

(3) An applicant who claims a name change by or under the common law of this State or any other state shall submit with the applicant's application the following:

(i) An affidavit of the name by which the applicant is known and transacts business, as demonstrated by a Social Security card or record together with documents from at least 2 of the following categories:

1. Tax records;

2. Selective Service card or records;

3. Voter registration card or records;

4. Passport;

5. A form of identification issued by a government unit that contains a photograph of the applicant;

6. Baptismal certificate;

7. Banking records; and

8. Other proof of age and identity that is satisfactory to the Administration;

(ii) Any document required under subparagraph (i) of this paragraph reflecting the legal name previously given to, or used by, the applicant prior to assuming the common law name;

(iii) Any driver's license issued to the applicant in the name previously used by the applicant prior to assuming the common law name; and

(iv) A copy of the applicant's birth certificate or other proof of age and identity that is satisfactory to the Administration.

Automobile Registration and Title

In order to change the name on your automobile registration and title, you will generally need to provide a copy of your name change court order, and fill out a state-specific form within a certain time period after the order has been signed. For example, Maryland requires its drivers whose names are changed by marriage or court order to apply for a corrected certificate of title within 30 days of the name change.

SOCIAL SECURITY ADMINISTRATION

If you change your name, it is very important that you notify the Social Security Administration as soon as practicable after your name change is official. You also need to inform your employer about your name change, so that your income is properly credited on your Social Security earnings record. If not, you will probably be faced with a lot of confusion and explaining to do in the future when you apply for Social Security benefits.

Applying for a New Social Security Card

After your name has been legally changed, you should obtain a new Social Security card from the Social Security Administration (SSA). You can obtain the necessary application forms from your local SSA office. You can find out the location of your nearest SSA office by calling 1-800-772-1213/1-800-325-0778 (TTY). In addition, you can obtain this information from the SSA website (http://www.ssa.gov/).

In order to obtain an amended social security card, you must file an Application for a Social Security Card. (Form SS-5). You will also have to provide certain documentation to prove your identity. You will need proof that shows your old name as well as your new name, such as a marriage certificate. If you were born outside the United States, you will also need to provide proof of your U.S. citizenship or that you are lawfully in the U.S.

You must file the application along with any required documents. You must submit original documents or copies certified by the custodian of the record. The SSA does not accept photocopies of documents, and notarized copies are not acceptable.

The completed form, along with the required supporting documents, can be mailed or taken to the nearest Social Security office. The SSA will return your original documents and issue you a new Social Security card which reflects your new name and the identical social security number you used prior to your name change.

A sample Application for a Social Security Card (Form SS-5) is set forth at Appendix 11.

Applying for a New Social Security Number

The Social Security Administration will not give you a new social security number just because you changed your name. However, if the reason you changed your name was because you were being harassed or you were trying to escape an abusive situation, you should be able to change your social security number on the same basis. Doing so will make it more difficult for the abusive person to locate you.

In order to obtain a new social security number, you should go to the local SSA office. You can also obtain information from the SSA website. In support of your request to change your social security number, you will be required to provide the SSA with the following documentation.

Proof of Identity

1. Proof of your name. If you have already changed your name, you will need to bring proof of your old name as well as proof of your new name.

2. Proof of your age, e.g. your driver's license.

3. Proof of your citizenship status, e.g., birth certificate for a U.S. citizen at birth; naturalization papers for a naturalized U.S. citizen; alien registration card for a permanent resident alien.

Proof of Custody

If you are also requesting that your child's social security number be changed, in addition to the documentation listed above, you need to provide proof that you have custody of your child.

Proof of Harassment or Abuse

If your request to change your social security number is based on harassment or abuse, you will also need to provide the following documentation, if applicable:

1. Police reports.

2. Medical records.

3. Restraining orders or orders of protection issued by a Court.

4. Letters from shelters stating that you stayed there due to harassment or abuse.

5. Letters from people who may have witnessed the harassment or abuse, or who may have provided you with shelter, such as family members and friends.

6. Names of social workers or counselors who are aware of the harassment or abuse.

7. Names of any other individual who had knowledge of the harassment or abuse.

U.S. PASSPORT AGENCY

If you have a valid U.S. passport, and you subsequently change your name, you must change your name on the passport or expect to run into a lot of difficulty next time you plan on traveling outside the

United States. In order to have your name officially changed and a new passport issued, you must complete a Passport Amendment/Validation Application (Form DS-19). This form should be used for amending a previously issued US passport whenever there is a change in the printed information, including a name change.

A sample Passport Amendment/Validation Application (Form DS-19) is set forth at Appendix 12.

You must complete, sign and date the application and include documentary evidence to support your name change, such as a certified court order or marriage certificate. The application and documentation, and your current U.S. Passport, should be mailed to the following address:

> Charleston Passport Center
> Attn: Amendments
> 1269 Holland Street
> Charleston, SC 29405

There is no fee to have a U.S. passport amended. Your amended U.S. passport and any documentary evidence submitted will be returned to you by first-class mail.

If your name has changed since your passport was issued and you do not have a legal document formally changing your name, or if your passport has expired prior to your name change, you must apply in person. The DOS has set up a website (http://iafdb.travel.state.gov/) where a customer can find the nearest passport agency. From the website, the customer can search using either their zip code, state, or state/city in order to obtain a list of the nearest designated passport facilities.

A directory of regional passport agencies is set forth at Appendix 13.

SELECTIVE SERVICE SYSTEM

If you are a male between the ages of 18 and 26, you are required to register with the Selective Service system, whether or not you are a U.S. citizen. If you legally change your name, you are required to send a copy of your petition and name change court order to the Selective Service within 20 days of the date the order was signed, along with Selective Service Form B, which is the tear-off "Change of Information" form every man receives in the mail with his registration acknowledgment card following registration. The documents should be mailed to the following address:

> Registration Information Office
> Selective Service System

P. O. Box 94638
Palatine, IL 60094-4638

The documents should be sent to the Selective Service System by certified mail, and you should request a return receipt. A copy of the receipt and a signed affidavit stating that you sent the documents to the Selective Service must generally be filed with the Court where the name change order was issued within a certain time period.

Corrections will take four to six weeks to process, after which you will be mailed an amended acknowledgement card which reflects your new name.

VOTER REGISTRATION SYSTEM

If you are a registered voter, you should change your name on your voter registration card so that there is no confusion when it comes time for you to vote. In general, you should send written notice of your name change, along with supporting documentation, such as your name change court order or marriage license, to the local voter registration board in the county where you are currently registered. If the board is satisfied with the proof of name change, your record will be amended.

Depending on the state in which you live, forms for changing your name on your voter registration may be available at your local Department of Motor Vehicles.

INTERNAL REVENUE SERVICE

The Internal Revenue Service (IRS) requires you to notify them of any address change. The IRS does not require you to notify them of your name change if you have not also changed your address. The IRS refers to Social Security records. Therefore, it is important that the name the Social Security Administration has in its system for your social security number agrees with the name on your tax return.

Following a legal name change, when preparing your annual tax return, use your new name and make sure you have already changed your Social Security record, as set forth above. The IRS records are generally updated 10 days after the records at the Social Security Administration are changed.

UNITED STATES CITIZENSHIP AND IMMIGRATION SERVICES

If you are a resident alien, naturalized citizen or non-resident alien, you must photocopy your petition and signed name change court order and file it with the United States Citizenship and Immigration Services (USCIS—formerly the INS) within a certain number of days after the order was signed.

You should send these documents by certified mail, and also request a receipt. A copy of the receipt and a signed affidavit stating that you sent the documents to the USCIS must generally be filed with the Court where the name change order was issued within a certain time period.

U.S. BANKRUPTCY COURT

If you declared and were granted bankruptcy prior to your name change, you are required to send a photocopy of your petition and name change court order to the U.S. Bankruptcy Court that granted you bankruptcy relief. These documents should be sent by certified mail, and you must also request a receipt. A copy of the receipt and a signed affidavit stating that you sent the documents to the appropriate U.S. Bankruptcy Court must generally be filed with the Court where the name change order was issued within a certain time period.

CRIMINAL JUSTICE SYSTEM

In general, if you were convicted of a crime, you will likely be required to send a photocopy of your petition and name change court order to the appropriate division of criminal justice within a certain time period after the order was signed. These documents should be sent by certified mail, and you must also request a receipt.

A copy of the receipt and a signed affidavit stating that you sent the documents to the appropriate criminal justice division must generally be filed with the Court where the name change order was issued within a certain time period.

MISCELLANEOUS NOTIFICATIONS

As discussed above, there are many government agencies and private businesses with whom an individual has contact. You should confer with the checklist in Appendix 7 to see if any of the entities listed apply to your situation, and follow up with a letter notifying these companies that your name has been legally changed. A copy of your supporting documentation should accompany the letter, e.g., court order, marriage certificate, divorce decree, etc.

A sample name change notification letter for this purpose is attached at Appendix 14.

APPENDIX 1:
DIRECTORY OF STATE CHANGE OF NAME LAWS

ALASKA

Chapter 09.55. SPECIAL ACTIONS AND PROCEEDINGS

Article 01. CHANGE OF NAME

Sec. 09.55.010. Jurisdiction in action for change of name.

A person may bring an action for change of name in the superior court. A change of name of a person may not be made unless the court finds sufficient reasons for the change and also finds it consistent with the public interest. A change of name upon marriage, dissolution, or divorce meets these requirements.

ARIZONA

Sec. 2-60112-601. Application; venue; judgment.

A. When a person desires to change his name and to adopt another name, he may file an application in the superior court in the county of his residence, setting forth reasons for the change of name and the name he wishes to adopt. The court may enter judgment that the adopted name of the party be substituted for the original name.

B. The parent, guardian ad litem or next friend of a minor may file an application for change of the name of the minor in the county of the minor's residence. The court shall consider the best interests of the child in determining whether to enter judgment that the name of the minor be changed.

Sec. 2-60212-602. Notice of application; effect of change on rights and obligations

A. If upon the filing of the application for change of name the court deems it proper that notice be given, it may order that notice of the application be given by publication or by service upon any party interested.

B. The change of name shall not operate to release the person from any obligations which he has incurred or is under by the original name, or defeat or destroy any rights of property or action which he had in his original name.

ARKANSAS

§ 9-2-101. Procedure.

(a) Upon the application of any person within the jurisdiction of the courts, the chancery and circuit courts shall have power, upon good reasons shown, to alter or change the name of the person.

(b) When application is made to the courts under this section, it shall be by petition, in writing, embodying the reasons for the application.

(c)(1) When allowed, the petition shall, by order of the court, be spread upon the record, together with the decree of the court.

(2) An appropriate order, as prescribed in this subsection, may be made by a chancellor or circuit judge in vacation. This order shall have the same force and effect as if made at term time.

§ 9-2-102. Use of new name.

Any person whose name may be so changed by judgment or decree of any of the courts shall afterward be known and designated, sue and be sued, plead and be impleaded, by the name thus conferred, except that records of persons under the jurisdiction and supervision of the Department of Correction shall continue to reflect the name as committed to the department's jurisdiction and supervision by the various circuit courts of the State of Arkansas.

CALIFORNIA

§ 1275 Civ. Proc.

Applications for change of names must be determined by the Superior Courts. (Amended by Stats. 1983, Ch. 486, Sec. 1.)

§ 1276 Civ. Proc.

All applications for change of names shall be made to the superior court of the county where the person whose name is proposed to be changed resides either (a) by petition signed by the person or, if the person is under 18 years of age, by one of the person's parents, if living, or if both parents are dead, then by the guardian of the person and, if there is no guardian, then by some near relative or friend of the person or (b) as provided in Section 7638 of the Family Code. The petition or pleading shall specify the place of birth and residence of the person, his or her present name, the name proposed, and the reason for the change of name, and shall, if neither parent of the person is living, name, as far as known to the person proposing the name change, the near relatives of the person, and their place of residence. In an action for a change of name commenced by the filing of a petition: (a) If the person whose name is proposed to be changed is under 18 years of age and the petition is signed by only one parent, the petition shall specify the address, if known, of the other parent if living. (b) If the person whose name is proposed to be changed is 12 years of age or over, has been relinquished to an adoption agency by his or her parent or parents, and has not been legally adopted, the petition shall be signed by the person and the adoption agency to which the person was relinquished. The near relatives of the person and their place of residence shall not be included in the petition unless they are known to the person whose name is proposed to be changed.

(a) Where an action for a change of name is commenced by the filing of a petition, the court shall thereupon make an order reciting the filing of the petition, the name of the person by whom it is filed and the name proposed, and directing all persons interested in the matter to appear before the court at a time and place specified, which shall be not less than four or more than eight weeks from the time of making the order, to show cause why the application for change of name should not be granted. A copy of the order to show cause shall be published pursuant to Section 6064 of the Government Code in a newspaper of general circulation to be designated in the order published in the county. If no newspaper of general circulation is published in the county, a copy of the order to show cause shall be posted by the clerk of the court in three of the most public places in the county in which the court is located, for a like period. Proof shall be made to the satisfaction of the court of this publication or posting, at the time of the hearing of the application. Four weekly publications shall be sufficient publication of the order to show cause. If the order is published in a daily newspaper, publication once a week for four successive weeks shall be sufficient. Where a petition has been filed for a minor and the other parent, if living, does not join in consenting thereto, the petitioner shall cause, not less than 30 days prior to the hearing, to be served notice of the time and place of the hearing or a copy of the order to show cause on the other parent pursuant to Section 413.10, 414.10,415.10, or 415.40.

§ 1279.5 Civ. Proc.

(a) Except as provided in subdivision (b), (c), (d), or (e), nothing in this title shall be construed to abrogate the common law right of any person to change his or her name.

COLORADO

Title 13 - Courts and Court Procedure

ARTICLE 15 - Change of Name

§ 13-15-101 - Petition - proceedings.

Every person desiring to change his name may present a petition to that effect, verified by affidavit, to the district or county court in the county of the petitioner's residence. The petition shall set forth the petitioner's full name, the new name desired, and a concise statement of the reason for such desired change. The court shall order such change to be made and spread upon the records of the court in proper form if the court is satisfied that the desired change would be proper and not detrimental to the interests of any other person.

§ 13-15-102 - Publication of change.

(1) Public notice of such change of name shall be given at least three times in a newspaper published in the county where such person is residing within twenty days after the order of the court is made, and, if no newspaper is published in that county, such notice shall be published in a newspaper in such county as the court directs.

(2) Public notice of such name change through publication as required in subsection (1) of this section shall not be required if the petitioner has been:

(a) The victim of a crime, the underlying factual basis of which has been found by the court on the record to include an act of domestic violence, as defined in section 18-6-800.3 (1), C.R.S.;

(b) The victim of child abuse, as defined in section 18-6-401, C.R.S.; or

(c) The victim of domestic abuse as that term is defined in section 14-4-101 (2), C.R.S.

CONNECTICUT

Sec. 52-11. Complaints for change of name.

The superior court in each judicial district shall have jurisdiction of complaints praying for a change of name, brought by any person residing in the judicial district, and may change the name of the complainant, who shall thereafter be known by the name prescribed by said court in its decree.

DELAWARE

Chapter 59. CHANGE OF NAME

(a) Any person who desires to change his or her name, shall present a petition, duly verified, to the Court of Common Pleas sitting in the county in which the person resides. The petition shall set forth such person's name and the name he or she desires to assume.

(b) Family Court shall have jurisdiction over a change of name as part of divorce proceedings or as part of the establishment of paternity under the Uniform Parentage Act.

(c) The common law right of any person to change his or her name is hereby abrogated as to individuals subject to the supervision of the State of Delaware Department of Correction. Such individuals may only effect a name change by petitioning the Court of Common Pleas as follows:

(1) Individuals subject to the supervision of the Department of Correction shall be prohibited from adopting any names other than their legal names or otherwise effecting name changes, except as provided in this subsection.

(2) When, based upon testimony or sworn affidavits, the court finds that a petition for a name change of an individual subject to the supervision of the Department of Correction is motivated by a sincerely held religious belief, the court may grant such petition. In any case in which an individual subject to the supervision of the Department of Correction petitions the Court of Common Pleas for a change of name, the Court shall provide notice and opportunity to oppose the name change to the Department of Correction and shall permit it to submit any appropriate documentation in support of its opposition.

(3) If an individual is granted a name change pursuant to paragraph 2 of this subsection, he or she must provide all names previously held or adopted, as well as his or her legal name when signing any legal document or providing information to a law enforcement officer.

(4) The granting of any name changes pursuant to this subsection shall not restrict the Department of Correction from maintaining institutional files or otherwise referring to individuals by the names under which they became subject to the Department's supervision.

§ 5902. Requirements for minor's petition.

If the name sought to be changed under this chapter is that of a minor, the petition shall be signed by at least one of the minor's parents, if there is a parent living, or if both parents are dead, by the legal guardian of such minor. When the minor is over the age of 14, the petition shall also be signed by the minor.

§ 5903. Publication of petition prior to filing.

No petition for change of name under this chapter shall be granted unless it affirmatively appears that the petition has been published in a newspaper published in the county in which the proceeding is had, at least once a week for 3 weeks before the petition is filed.

§ 5904. Determination by Court.

Upon presentation of a petition for change of name under this chapter, and it appearing that the requirements of this chapter have been fully complied with, and there appearing no reason for not granting the petition, the prayer of the petition may be granted.

DISTRICT OF COLUMBIA

Title 16 Particular Actions, Proceedings and Matters

Chapter 25 Change of Name

§ 16-2501. Application; persons who may file.

Whoever, being a resident of the District and desiring a change of name, may file an application in the Superior Court setting forth the reasons therefor and also the name desired to be assumed. If the applicant is an infant, the application shall be filed by his parent, guardian, or next friend.

§ 16-2502. Notice; contents.

Prior to a hearing pursuant to this chapter, notice of the filing of the application, containing the substance and prayer thereof, shall be published once a week for three consecutive weeks in a newspaper in general circulation published in the District.

§ 16-2503. Decree.

On proof of the notice prescribed by section 16-2502, and upon a showing that the court deems satisfactory, the court may change the name of the applicant according to the prayer of the application.

FLORIDA

§ 68.07 Change of name.

(1) Chancery courts have jurisdiction to change the name of any person residing in this state on petition of the person filed in the county in which he or she resides.

(2) The petition shall be verified and show:

(a) That petitioner is a bona fide resident of and domiciled in the county where the change of name is sought.

(b) If known, the date and place of birth of petitioner, petitioner's father's name, mother's maiden name, and where petitioner has resided since birth.

(c) If petitioner is married, the name of petitioner's spouse and if petitioner has children, the names and ages of each and where they reside.

(d) If petitioner's name has previously been changed and when and where and by what court.

(e) Petitioner's occupation and where petitioner is employed and has been employed for 5 years next preceding filing of the petition. If petitioner owns and operates a business, the name and place of it shall be stated and petitioner's connection therewith and how long petitioner has been identified with said business. If petitioner is in a profession, the profession shall be stated, where the petitioner has practiced the profession and if a graduate of a school or schools, the name or names thereof, time of graduation, and degrees received.

(f) Whether the petitioner has been generally known or called by any other names and if so, by what names and where.

(g) Whether petitioner has ever been adjudicated a bankrupt and if so, where and when.

(h) Whether petitioner has ever been convicted of a felony and if so, when and where.

(i) Whether any money judgment has ever been entered against petitioner and if so, the name of the judgment creditor, the amount and date thereof, the court by which entered, and whether the judgment has been satisfied.

(j) That the petition is filed for no ulterior or illegal purpose and granting it will not in any manner invade the property rights of others, whether partnership, patent, good will, privacy, trademark, or otherwise.

(k) That the petitioner's civil rights have never been suspended, or if the petitioner's civil rights have been suspended, that full restoration of civil rights has occurred.

(3) The hearing on the petition may be immediately after it is filed.

(4) On filing the final judgment, the clerk shall, if the birth occurred in this state, send a report of the judgment to the Office of Vital Statistics of the Department of Health on a form to be furnished by the department. The form shall contain sufficient information to identify the original birth certificate of the person, the new name, and the file number of the judgment. This report shall be filed by the department with respect to a person born in this state and shall become a part of the vital statistics of this state. With respect to a person born in another state, the clerk shall provide the petitioner with a certified copy of the final judgment.

(5) If the petitioner is a convicted felon, the clerk must, upon the filing of the final judgment, send a report of the judgment to the Florida Department of Law Enforcement on a form to be furnished by that department. The report must contain sufficient information to identify the original criminal record of the petitioner, the new name of the petitioner, and the file number of the judgment. With respect to a person convicted of a felony in another state or of a federal offense, the Florida Department of Law Enforcement must send the report to the respective state's office of law enforcement records or to the office of the Federal Bureau of Investigation.

(6) A husband and wife and minor children may join in one petition for change of name and the petition shall show the facts required of a petitioner as to the husband and wife and the names of the minor children may be changed at the discretion of the court.

(7) When only one parent petitions for a change of name of a minor child, process shall be served on the other parent and proof of such service shall be filed in the cause; provided, however, that where the other parent is a nonresident, constructive notice of the petition may be given pursuant to chapter 49, and proof of publication shall be filed in the cause without the necessity of recordation.

(8) Nothing herein applies to any change of name in proceedings for dissolution of marriage or for adoption of children.

GEORGIA

19-12-1. Petition for name change; notice of filing; consent of minor's parents or guardian; service on parents or guardian; time of hearing; judgment; clerk's fees.

(a) Any person desirous of changing his name or the name or names of his minor child or children may present a petition to the superior court of the county of his residence, setting forth fully and particularly the reasons why the change is asked, which petition shall be verified by the petitioner.

(b) Within seven days of the filing of the petition, the petitioner shall cause a notice of the filing, signed by him, to be published in the official legal organ of the county once a week for four weeks. The notice shall contain therein the name of the petitioner, the name of the person whose name is to be changed if different from that of the petitioner, the new name desired, the court in which the petition is pending, the date on which the petition was filed, and the right of any interested or affected party to appear and file objections.

(c) If the petition seeks to change the name of a minor child, the written consent of his parent or parents if they are living and have not abandoned the child, or the written consent of the child's guardian if both parents are dead or have abandoned the child, shall be filed with the petition, except that the written consent of a parent shall not be required if the parent has not contributed to the support of the child for a continuous period of five years or more immediately preceding the filing of the petition.

(d) In all cases, before a minor child's name may be changed, the parent or parents of the child shall be served with a copy of the petition. If the parent or parents reside within this state, service of the petition shall be made in person, except that if the location or address of the parent is unknown, service of the petition on the parent shall be made by publication as provided in this Code section. If the parent or parents reside outside this state, service of the petition on the parent or parents residing outside this state shall be made by certified mail if the address is known or by publication as provided in this Code section if the address is not known.

(e) Where a child resides with persons other than his parent or parents, a copy of the petition shall be served upon the person acting as guardian of the child in the same manner as service would be made on a parent.

(f) Upon the expiration of: (1) Thirty days from the filing of the petition if the person whose name to be changed is an adult; (2) Thirty days from the date of service upon the parent, parents, or guardian of a minor whose name is to be changed if the parent, parents, or guardian reside within this state; or (3) Sixty days from the date of service upon the parent, parents, or guardian of a minor whose name is to be changed if either the parent, parents, or guardian reside outside the state and the petition is served by mail, and after proof to the court of publication of the notice as required in this Code section is made, if no objection is filed, the court shall proceed at chambers at such date as the court shall fix to hear and determine all matters raised by the petition and to render final judgment or decree thereon. For such service, the clerk shall receive the fees prescribed in Code Section 15-6-77, relating to fees of clerks of the superior courts for civil cases.

19-12-2. Hearing on objections to petition.

If written objections are filed by any interested or affected party within the time limits specified in subsection (f) of Code Section 19-12-1, the court shall thereupon proceed to hear the matter at chambers.

19-12-3. Certificate of change of name; use as evidence; form of certificate.

(a) At any time after the entry of the final order of change of name, upon the request of the petitioner requesting the change of name, the clerk of the court granting the same shall issue to the petitioner a certificate of change of name, under the seal of the court, upon payment to the clerk of the fee provided in paragraph (4) of subsection (g) of Code Section 15-6-77. The certificate shall be received as evidence of the facts contained in the certificate.

(b) The certificate of change of name shall be in substantially the following form:

This is to certify that _____ (name of petitioner) has obtained final order of change of name in the Superior Court of _____ County, Georgia, on the _____ day of _____, _____, as shown by the records of the court. The name (or names) of _____ (full name prior to entry of the final order of change of name) has (or have) been changed to _____ (full name after entry of the final order of change of name). Given under the hand and seal of said court, this the _____day of _____, _____. (Seal of court) _____ Clerk

Georgia Code 19-12-4. Change of name with fraudulent intent not authorized.

Nothing contained in this chapter shall authorize any person to change his name with a view to deprive another fraudulently of any right under the law.

HAWAII

§574-5 Change of Name Procedure.

(a) It shall be unlawful to change any name adopted or conferred under this chapter, except:

(1) Upon an order of the lieutenant governor;

(2) By a final order, decree, or judgment of the family court issued as follows:

(A) When in an adoption proceeding a change of name of the person to be adopted is requested and the court includes the change of name in the adoption decree;

(B) When in a divorce proceeding either party to the proceeding requests to resume the middle name or names and the last name used by the party prior to the marriage or a middle name or names and last name declared and used during any prior marriage and the court includes the change of names in the divorce decree; or

(C) When in a proceeding for a change of name of a legitimate or legitimated minor initiated by one parent, the family court, upon proof that the parent initiating the name change has made all reasonable efforts to locate and notify the other parent of the name change proceeding but has not been able to locate, notify, or elicit a response from the other parent, and after an appropriate hearing, orders a change of name determined to be in the best interests of the minor; provided that the family court may waive the notice requirement to the non-initiating, non-custodial parent where the court finds that the waiver is necessary for the protection of the minor;

(3) Upon marriage pursuant to section 574-1;

(4) Upon legitimation pursuant to section 338-21; or

(5) By an order or decree of any court of competent jurisdiction within any state of the United States, the District of Columbia, the

Commonwealth of Puerto Rico, or any territory or possession of the United States, changing the name of a person born in this State.

(b) The order of change of name by the lieutenant governor shall be founded upon a notarized petition. The petition shall be executed by the person desirous of making the change of name. In the case of a minor, the petition shall be executed:

(1) By the parents;

(2) By the parent who has custody of the minor with the notarized consent of the noncustodial parent; or

(3) By the guardian of the person of the minor.

(c) The filing fee of $100 shall accompany the petition when submitted and shall not be refundable.

(d) A notice of change of name signed by the lieutenant governor shall be published once in a newspaper of general circulation in the State as mentioned in the order for change of name, and the petitioner within sixty days of the signing of the notice of change of name shall deposit at the office of the lieutenant governor an affidavit executed by an officer of the newspaper publishing the notice showing that the notice has been published therein. The affidavit shall have attached to it a clipping showing the notice as published. Failure to deposit the affidavit of publication as required shall void that petition for a change of name by that petitioner.

(e) When the petition is accompanied by an affidavit executed by a prosecuting attorney of this State, the affidavit shall show that for the protection of the person desirous of making a change of name, the following actions shall not be necessary:

(1) Publication in a newspaper of general circulation in the State; and

(2) Recordation in the bureau of conveyances.

IDAHO

TITLE 7 SPECIAL PROCEEDINGS - CHAPTER 8 CHANGE OF NAMES

7-801. JURISDICTION IN DISTRICT COURT.

Application for change of names must be heard and determined by the district courts.

7-802. PETITION FOR CHANGE.

All applications for change of names must be made to the district court of the county where the person whose name is proposed to be changed resides, by petition, signed by such person; and if such person is under the age of eighteen (18) years, by one (1) of the parents, if living; or if both be dead, then by the guardian; and if there be no guardian, then by some near relative or friend. The petition must specify the place of birth and residence of such person, his or her present same, the name proposed, and reason for such change of name, and must, if the father of such person be not living, name, as far as known to the petitioner, the near relatives of such person, and their place of residence.

7-803. PUBLICATION OF PETITION.

A notice of hearing of such petition signed by the clerk and issued under the seal of the court, must be published for four (4) successive weeks in some newspaper printed in the county, if a newspaper be printed therein, but if no newspaper be printed in the county a copy of such notice of hearing must be posted at three [(3)] of the most public places in the county for a like period, and proofs must be made of such publication or posting before the petition can be considered. The notice of hearing may be substantially in the following form:

NOTICE OF HEARING

In the District Court of the ____ Judicial District of the State of Idaho in and for ____ County.

In the matter of the application of ____ for change in name.

(Assertions herein contained refer to assertions in the petition)

A petition by ____, born ____ at ____ now residing at ____ proposing a change in name to ____ has been filed in the above entitled court, the reason for the change in name being _____

the name of the petitioner's father is ____ address ____ (if living); the

names and addresses of petitioner's near relatives (if father be dead) are:

_____

_____

_____

such petition will be heard at such time as the court may appoint, and objections may be filed by any person who can, in such objections, show to the court a good reason against such a change of name.

WITNESS my hand and seal of said District Court this ___ day of ___

20___

____ Attorney for petitioner

____ Residence or post office address

7-804. (R) HEARING AND ORDER.

Such application must be heard at such time during term as the court may appoint, and objections may be filed by any person who can, in such objections, show to the court good reason against such change of name. On the hearing the court may examine, upon oath, any of the petitioners, remonstrants or other persons touching the application, and may make an order changing the name or dismissing the application, as to the court may seem right and proper.

ILLINOIS

Illinois Statutes

735 IL CS 5/21-101 Proceedings; parties.

If any person who is a resident of this State and has resided in this State for 6 months desires to change his or her name and to assume another name by which to be afterwards called and known, the person may file a petition in the circuit court of the county wherein he or she resides praying for that relief. If it appears to the court that the conditions herein aftermentioned have been complied with and that there is no reason why the prayer should not be granted, the court, by an order to be entered of record, may direct and provide that the name of that person be changed in accordance with the prayer in the petition. The filing of a petition in accordance with this Section shall be the sole and exclusive means by which any person committed under the laws of this State to a penal institution may change his or her name and assume another name. However, any person convicted of a felony, misdemeanor criminal sexual abuse when the victim of the offense at the time of its commission is under 18 years of age, misdemeanor sexual exploitation of a child, misdemeanor indecent solicitation of a child, or misdemeanor indecent solicitation of an adult in this State or any other state who has not been pardoned may not file a petition for a name change until 2 years have passed since completion and discharge from his or her sentence. A petitioner may include his or her spouse and adult unmarried children, with their consent, and his or her minor children where it appears to the court that it is for their best interest, in the petition and prayer, and the court's order shall then include the spouse and children. Whenever any minor has resided in the family of any person for the space of 3 years and has been recognized and known as an adopted child in the family of that person, the application herein provided for may be made by the person having that minor in his or her family. An order shall be entered as to a minor only if the court finds by clear and convincing evidence that the change is necessary to serve the best interest of the child. In determining the best interest of a minor child under this Section, the court shall consider all relevant factors, including:

(1) The wishes of the child's parents and any person acting as a parent who has physical custody of the child.

(2) The wishes of the child and the reasons for those wishes. The court may interview the child in chambers to ascertain the child's wishes with respect to the change of name. Counsel shall be present at the interview unless otherwise agreed upon by the parties. The court shall cause a court reporter to be present who shall make a complete record of the interview instantaneously to be part of the record in the case.

(3) The interaction and interrelationship of the child with his or her parents or persons acting as parents who have physical custody of the child, step-parents, siblings, step-siblings, or any other person who may significantly affect the child's best interest.

(4) The child's adjustment to his or her home, school, and community.

735 IL CS 5/21-102 Petition.

The petition shall set forth the name then held, the name sought to be assumed, the residence of the petitioner, the length of time the petitioner has resided in this State, and the state or country of the petitioner's nativity or supposed nativity. The petition shall be signed by the person petitioning or, in case of minors, by the parent or guardian having the legal custody of the minor. The petition shall be verified by the affidavit of some credible person.

735 IL CS 5/21-103 Notice by publication.

(a) Previous notice shall be given of the intended application by publishing a notice thereof in some newspaper published in the municipality in which the person resides if the municipality is in a county with a population under 2,000,000, or if the person does not reside in a municipality in a county with a population under 2,000,000,or if no newspaper is published in the municipality or if the person resides in a county with a population of 2,000,000 or more, then in some newspaper published in the county where the person resides, or if no newspaper is published in that county, then in some convenient newspaper published in this State. The notice shall be inserted for 3consecutive weeks, the first insertion to be at least 6 weeks before the return day upon which the petition is to be filed, and shall be signed by the petitioner or, in case of a minor, the minor's parent or guardian, and shall set forth the return day of court on which the petition is to be filed and the name sought to be assumed.

INDIANA

IC 34-28-2 Chapter 2. Change of Name

IC 34-28-2-1

Sec. 1. Except as provided in section 1.5 of this chapter, the circuit courts in Indiana may change the names of natural persons on application by petition. As added by P.L.1-1998, SEC.24. Amended by P.L.18-1998, SEC.1. IC 34-28-2-1.5

Sec. 1.5. A person may not petition for a change of name under this chapter if the person is confined to a department of correction facility. As added by P.L.18-1998, SEC.2. IC 34-28-2-2

Sec. 2. (a) The petition described in section (1) of this chapter may be filed with the circuit court of the county in which the person resides.

(b) In the case of a parent or guardian who wishes to change the name of a minor child, the petition must be verified, and it must state in detail the reason the change is requested. In addition, except where a parent's consent is not required under IC 31-19-9, the written consent of a parent, or the written consent of the guardian if both parents are dead, must be filed with the petition.

(c) Before a minor child's name may be changed, the parents or guardian of the child must be served with a copy of the petition as required by the Indiana trial rules. As added by P.L.1-1998, SEC.24. IC 34-28-2-3

Sec. 3. (a) Upon filing a petition for a name change, the applicant shall give notice of the petition as follows:

(1) By three (3) weekly publications in a newspaper of general circulation published in the county in which the petition is filed in court.

(2) If no newspaper is published in the county in which the petition is filed, the applicant shall give notice in a newspaper published nearest to that county in an adjoining county.

(3) The last weekly publication shall be published not less than thirty (30) days before the day the petition will be heard as indicated in the notice.

(b) In the case of a petition described in section 2(b) of this chapter, the petitioner must publish the first notice of the petition not more than seven (7) days after the date the petition is filed.

(c) In the case of a petition described in section 2(b) of this chapter, the notice required by this section must include the following:

(1) The name of the petitioner.

(2) The name of the minor child whose name is to be changed.

(3) The new name desired.

(4) The name of the court in which the action is pending.

(5) The date on which the petition was filed.

(6) A statement that any person has the right to appear at the hearing and to file objections.

(d) Except as provided in section 1.5 of this chapter, in the case of a person who has had a felony conviction within ten (10) years before filing a petition for a change of name, at least thirty (30) days before the hearing the petitioner must give notice of the filing of the petition to:

(1) the sheriff of the county in which the petitioner resides;

(2) the prosecuting attorney of the county in which the petitioner resides; and

(3) the Indiana central repository for criminal history information.

(e) The notice given to the Indiana central repository for criminal history information under subsection (d) must include the petitioner's full current name, requested name change, date of birth, address, physical description, and a full set of classifiable fingerprints.

(f) The Indiana central repository for criminal history information shall forward a copy of any criminal records of the petitioner to the court for the court's information.

(g) A copy of the court decree granting or denying such a petition shall be sent to the Indiana state police.

(h) A person who violates subsection (d) commits a Class A misdemeanor.

Sec. 4. (a) Proof of the publication required in this chapter is made by filing a copy of the published notice, verified by the affidavit of a disinterested person, and when proof of publication is made, the court shall, subject to the limitations imposed by subsections (b), (c), and (d), proceed to hear the petition and make an order and decree the court determines is just and reasonable.

(b) In the case of a petition described in section 2(b) of this chapter, the court may not hear the petition and issue a final decree until after thirty (30) days from the later of:

(1) the filing of proof of publication of the notice required under subsection (a); or

(2) the service of the petition upon the parents or guardian of the minor child.

(c) In the case of a petition described in section 2(b) of this chapter, the court shall set a date for a hearing on the petition if:

(1) written objections have been filed; or

(2) either parent or the guardian of the minor child has refused or failed to give written consent as described in section 2(b) of this chapter.

The court shall require that appropriate notice of the hearing be given to the parent or guardian of the minor child or to any person who has filed written objections.

(d) In deciding on a petition to change the name of a minor child, the court shall be guided by the best interest of the child rule under IC 31-17-2-8. However, there is a presumption in favor of a parent of a minor child who:

(1) has been making support payments and fulfilling other duties in accordance with a decree issued under IC 31-15, IC 31-16, or IC 17 (or IC 31-1-11.5 before its repeal); and

(2) objects to the proposed name change of the child.

(e) In the case of a person required to give notice under section 3(d) of this chapter, the petitioner must certify to the court that the petitioner has complied with the notice requirements of that subsection.

Sec. 5. (a) A copy of the decree of the court changing the name of any natural person, certified under the seal of the court by the clerk of the court, is sufficient evidence of the name of the person, and of a change having been made, in any court of Indiana.

(b) In the case of a petition described in section 2(b) of this chapter, the court shall send a copy of the final decree to the state department of health and to the local health department of the county.

(c) In the case of a petition filed by a person at least seventeen (17) years of age, the court shall send a copy of the final decree to the clerk of the circuit court or board of registration of the county where the person resides.

IOWA

674.1 Authorization.

A person who has attained the age of majority and who does not have any civil disabilities may apply to the court to change the person's name by filing a verified petition as provided in this chapter. The verified petition may request a name change for minor children of the petitioner as well as the petitioner or a parent may file a verified petition requesting a name change on behalf of a minor child of the parent.

674.2 Petition to court.

The verified petition shall be addressed to the district court of the county where the applicant resides and shall state and provide for each person seeking a name change:

1. The name at the time the petition is filed of the person whose name is to be changed and the person's county of residence. If the person whose name is to be changed is a minor child, the petition shall state the name of the petitioner and the petitioner's relationship to the minor child.

2. A description including height, weight, color of hair, color of eyes, race, sex, and date and place of birth.

3. Residence at time of petition and any prior residences for the past five years.

4. Reason for change of name, briefly and concisely stated.

5. A legal description of all real property in this state owned by the petitioner.

6. The name the petitioner proposes to take.

7. A certified copy of the birth certificate to be attached to the petition.

674.3 Petition copy.

A copy of the petition shall be filed by the clerk of court with the division for records and statistics of the Iowa department of public health.

674.4 When granted.

A decree of change of name may be granted any time after thirty days of the filing of the petition. Section History: Early form

674.5 Contents of decree.

The decree shall describe the petitioner, giving the petitioner's name and former name, height, weight, color of hair, color of eyes, race, sex, date and place of birth and the given name of the spouse and any minor children affected by the change. The decree shall also give a legal description of all real property owned by the petitioner.

674.6 Notice—consent.

If the petitioner is married, the petitioner must give legal notice to the spouse, in the manner of an original notice, of the filing of the petition.

If the petition includes or is filed on behalf of a minor child fourteen years of age or older, the child's written consent to the change of name of that child is required. If the petition includes or is filed on behalf of a minor child under fourteen, both parents as stated on the birth certificate of the minor child shall file their written consent to the name change. If one of the parents does not consent to the name change, a hearing shall be set on the petition on twenty days' notice to the non-consenting parent pursuant to the rules of civil procedure. At the hearing the court may waive the requirement of consent as to one of the parents if it finds:

1. That the parent has abandoned the child;

2. That the parent has been ordered to contribute to the support of the child or to financially aid in the child's birth and has failed to do so without good cause; or

3. That the parent does not object to the name change after having been given due and proper notice. Section History: Early form [C73, 75, 77, 79, 81, § 674.6; 81 Acts, ch 201, § 3]

674.13 Further change barred.

A person shall not change the person's name more than once under this chapter unless just cause is shown. However, in a decree dissolving a person's marriage, the person's name may be changed back to the name appearing on the person's original birth certificate or to a legal name previously acquired in a former marriage.

KANSAS

Chapter 60.— PROCEDURE, CIVIL

Article 14.— CHANGE OF NAME

60-1401. Jurisdiction and costs.

The district court shall have authority to change the name of any person, township, town or city within this state at the cost of the petitioner without affecting any legal right.

60-1402. Change of name of person; notice; order.

(a) Petition. A petition may be filed in the county in which the petitioner resides stating: (1) That the petitioner has been a resident of the state for at least 60 days, (2) the reason for the change of name, and (3) the name desired.

(b) Notice. Service of notice of the hearing may be made either by mail or by publication, in the discretion of the court. If notice is directed by publication, such notice shall be published as provided in subsection (d) of K.S.A. 60-307, and amendments thereto; and if notice of hearing is directed to be given by mail, service of notice may be made by registered or certified mail to parties of interest, as prescribed by the court.

(c) Order. If upon hearing the judge is satisfied as to the truth of the allegations of the petition, and that there is reasonable cause for changing the name of the petitioner the judge shall so order.

60-1403. Municipalities.

A petition for the change of name of any township, town, or city may be filed in the district court of such county, signed by a majority of the legal voters of such body, setting forth the cause why such change is desirable and the name to be substituted. The court, upon being satisfied by proof that the prayer of the petitioners is just and reasonable, that notice as required in the foregoing section has been given, that the petitioners are legal voters of such township, town, or city and that they desire the change, and that such change will not result in an objectionable confusion of names within the state, may order the change prayed for in such petition.

KENTUCKY

401.010 Who may have name changed.

Any person at least eighteen (18) years of age may have his name changed by the District Court of the county in which he resides. If he resides on a United States Army post, military reservation or fort his name may be changed by the District Court of any county adjacent thereto. Effective: January 2, 1978

401.020 Child, who may have name changed.

Both parents, provided both are living, or one (1) parent if one (1) is deceased, or if no parent is living, the guardian, may have the name of a child under the age of eighteen (18) changed by the District Court of the county in which the child resides. However, if one (1) parent refuses or is unavailable to execute the petition, proper notice of filing the petition shall be served in accordance with the Rules of Civil Procedure. If the child resides on a United States Army post, military reservation or fort his name may be changed by the District Court of any county adjacent thereto.

401.030 Facts shown on order book of court.

The original name, age and place of birth, the name to which the change is made, and the names of the infant's father and mother, if known, and of the person on whose motion the change is made shall be entered on the order book of the District Court.

401.040 Certification of order for name change — Index kept by county clerk.

(1) If the District Court orders any person's name to be changed under this chapter, a copy of the order shall be certified by the clerk of that court to the county clerk, for record.

(2) The county clerk shall keep an alphabetical index for each book of records, referring to the page on which each person's name change appears, and giving the name from and to which it is changed.

LOUISIANA

PART IV. CHANGE OF NAME

§4751. Petition for name change; adults; minors

A. The name of a person may be changed as provided in this Section.

B. Whenever any person who has attained the age of majority desires to change his name, he shall present a petition to the district court of the parish of his residence or, in the case of a person incarcerated in a penal institution, to the district court of the parish in which he was sentenced, setting forth the reasons for the desired change.

C. If the person desiring such change is a minor or if the parents or parent or the tutor of the minor desire to change the name of the minor:

(1) The petition shall be signed by the father and mother of the minor or by the survivor in case one of them be dead.

(2) If one parent has been granted custody of the minor by a court of competent jurisdiction, the consent of the other parent is not necessary if the other parent has been served with a copy of the petition and any of the following exists:

(a) The other parent has refused or failed to comply with a court order of support for a period of one year.

(b) The other parent has failed to support the child for a period of three years after judgment awarding custody to the parent signing the petition.

(c) The other parent is not paying support and has refused or failed to visit, communicate, or attempt to communicate with the child without just cause for a period of two years.

(d) The other parent has refused or failed to visit, communicate, or attempt to communicate with the child without just cause for a period of ten years.

(3) In case the minor has no father or mother living, the petition shall be signed by the tutor or tutrix of the minor and in default of any tutor or tutrix, shall be signed by a special tutor appointed by the judge for that purpose.

(4) The petition may be signed by either the mother or the father acting alone if a child has been given a surname which is different from that authorized in R.S. 40:34(B)(1)(a).

D.(1) A person who has been convicted of a felony shall not be entitled to petition for a change of name under the provisions of this Section until his sentence has been satisfied. This Subsection shall apply whether the offender is actually imprisoned or on probation or parole.

(2) Notwithstanding the provisions of Paragraph (1) of this Subsection or any other provision of law to the contrary, a person convicted of any felony enumerated in R.S. 14:2(13) shall not be entitled to petition for a change of name.

MASSACHUSETTS

Chapter 210: Section 12. Petitions for change of name.

Section 12. A petition for the change of name of a person may be heard by the probate court in the county where the petitioner resides. The change of name of a person shall be granted unless such change is inconsistent with public interests.

Chapter 210: Section 13. Notice and certificate; decree; entry; conditions precedent.

Section 13. The court shall, before decreeing a change of name, request a report from the commissioner of probation on the person filing the petition and, except for good cause shown, require public notice of the petition to be given and any person may be heard thereon, and, upon entry of a decree, the name as established thereby shall be the legal name of the petitioner, and the register may issue a certificate, under the seal of the court, of the name as so established.

No decree shall be entered, however, until there has been filed in the court a copy of the birth record of the person whose name is sought to be changed and, in case such person's name has previously been changed by decree of court or at marriage pursuant to section one D of chapter forty-six, either a copy of the record of his birth amended to conform to the previous decree changing his name, a copy of such decree, or a copy of the record of marriage; provided, that the filing of any such copy may be dispensed with if the judge is satisfied that it cannot be obtained.

Chapter 210: Section 14. Annual return of changes.

Section 14. Each register of probate shall annually, in December, make a return to the commissioner of public health and the commissioner of probation of all changes of name made in his court.

MARYLAND

Rule 15-901. Action for change of name.

(a) Applicability.—This Rule applies to actions for change of name other than in connection with an adoption or divorce.

(b) Venue.—An action for change of name shall be brought in the county where the person whose name is sought to be changed resides.

(c) Petition.—(1) Contents.—The action for change of name shall be commenced by filing a petition captioned "In the Matter of . . ." [stating the name of the person whose name is sought to be changed] "for change of name to . . ." [stating the change of name desired]. The petition shall be under oath and shall contain at least the following information; (A) the name, address, and date and place of birth of the person whose name is sought to be; (B) whether the person whose name is sought to be changed has ever been known by any other name and, if so, the name or names and the circumstances under which they were used; (C) the change of name desired; (D) all reasons for the requested change; (E) a certification that the petitioner is not requesting the name change for any illegal or fraudulent purpose; and (F) if the person whose name is sought to be changed is a minor, the names and addresses of that person's parents and any guardian or custodian. (2) Documents to be attached to petition.—The petitioner shall attach to the petition a copy of a birth certificate or other documentary evidence from which the court can find that the current name of the person whose name is sought to be changed is as alleged.

(d) Service of petition.—When required.—If the person whose name is sought to be changed is a minor, a copy of the petition, any attachments, and the notice issued pursuant to section (e) of this Rule shall be served upon that person's parents and any guardian or custodian in the manner provided by Rule 2-121. When proof is made by affidavit that good faith efforts to serve a parent, guardian, or custodian pursuant to Rule 2-121 (a) have not succeeded and that Rule 2-121 (b) is inapplicable or that service pursuant to that Rule is impracticable, the court may order that service may be made by (1) the publication required by subsection (e)(2) of this Rule and (2) mailing a copy of the petition, any attachments, and notice by first class mail to the last known address of the parent, guardian, or custodian to be served.

(e) Notice.—(1) Issued by clerk.—Upon the filing of the petition, the clerk shall sign and issue a notice that (A) includes the caption of the action, (B) describes the substance of the petition and the relief sought, and (C) states the latest date by which an objection to the petition may be filed. (2) Publication.—Unless the court on motion of the petitioner orders otherwise, the notice shall be published one time in a newspaper of general circulation in the county at least fifteen days before the date specified in the notice for filing an objection to the petition. The petitioner shall thereafter file a certificate of publication.

(f) Objection to petition.—Any person may file an objection to the petition. The objection shall be filed within the time specified in the notice and shall be supported by an affidavit which sets forth the reasons for the objection. The affidavit shall be made on personal knowledge, shall set forth facts that would be admissible in evidence, and shall show affirmatively that the affiant is competent to testify to the matters stated in the affidavit. The objection and affidavit shall be served upon the petitioner in accordance with Rule 1-321. The petitioner may file a response within 15 days after being served with the objection and affidavit. A person desiring a hearing shall so request in the objection or response under the heading "Request for Hearing."

(g) Action by court.—After the time for filing objections and responses has expired, the court may hold a hearing or may rule on the petition without a hearing and shall enter an appropriate order, except that the court shall not deny the petition without a hearing if one was requested by the petitioner.

MAINE

§ 1-701. Petition to change name

If a person desires to have that person's name changed, the person may petition the judge of probate in the county where the person resides; or, if the person is a minor, that person's legal custodian may petition in the person's behalf, and the judge, after due notice, may change the name of the person and shall make and preserve a record of the name change. The fee for filing the petition is $25.

MICHIGAN

MICHIGAN COMPILED LAWS

711.1. Change of name; procedure, minors Sec. 1.

(1) The family division of the circuit court, or until January 1, 1998, the probate court, for a county may enter an order to change the name of a person who has been a resident of the county for not less than 1 year and who in accordance with subsection (2) petitions in writing to the court for that purpose showing a sufficient reason for the proposed change and that the change is not sought with any fraudulent intent. If the person who petitions for a name change has a criminal record, the person is presumed to be seeking a name change with a fraudulent intent. The burden of proof is on a petitioner who has a criminal record to rebut the presumption. The court shall set a time and place for hearing and order publication as provided by supreme court rule.

(2) A person who is 22 years of age or older and who petitions to have his or her name changed shall have 2 complete sets of his or her fingerprints taken at a local police agency. The fingerprints, along with a copy of the petition and the required processing fees, shall be forwarded to the department of state police. The department of state police shall compare those fingerprints with its records and shall forward a complete set of fingerprints to the federal bureau of investigation for a comparison with the records available to that agency. The department of state police shall report to the court in which the petition is filed the information contained in the department's records with respect to any pending charges against the petitioner or any record of conviction of the petitioner and shall report to the court similar information obtained from the federal bureau of investigation. If there are no pending charges against the petitioner or any record of conviction against the petitioner, the department of state police shall destroy its copy of the petitioner's fingerprints. The court shall not act upon the petition for a name change until the department of state police reports the information required by this subsection to the court.

(3) If the court enters an order to change the name of a person who has a criminal record, the court shall forward the order to the central records division of the Michigan state police and to 1 or more of the following: (a) The department of corrections if the person named in the order is in prison or on parole or has been imprisoned or released from parole in the immediately preceding 2 years. (b) The sheriff of the county in which the person named in the order was last convicted if the person was incarcerated in a county jail or released from a county jail within the immediately preceding 2 years. (c) The court that has juris-

diction over the person named in the order if the person named in the order is under the jurisdiction of the family division of the circuit court, or until January 1, 1998, the probate court, or has been discharged from the jurisdiction of that court within the immediately preceding 2 years.

(4) The court may permit a person having the same name, or a similar name to that which the petitioner proposes to assume, to intervene in the proceeding for the purpose of showing fraudulent intent.

(5) Except as provided in subsection (7), if the petitioner is a minor, the petition shall be signed by the mother and father jointly; by the surviving parent if 1 is deceased; if both parents are deceased, by the guardian of the minor; or by1 of the minor's parents if there is only 1 legal parent available to give consent. If either parent has been declared mentally incompetent, the petition may be signed by the guardian for that parent. The written consent to the change of name of a minor 14 years of age or older, signed by the minor in the presence of the court, shall be filed with the court before any order changing the name of the minor is entered. If the court considers the child to be of sufficient age to express a preference, the court shall consult a minor under 14 years of age as to a change in his or her name, and the court shall consider the minor's wishes.

(6) If the petitioner is married, the court, in its order changing the name of the petitioner, may include the name of the spouse, if the spouse consents, and may include the names of minor children of the petitioner of whom the petitioner has legal custody. The written consent to the change of name of a child 14 years of age or older, signed by the child in the presence of the court, shall be filed with the court before the court includes that child in its order. Except as provided in subsection (7), the name of a minor under 14 years of age may not be changed unless he or she is the natural or adopted child of the petitioner and unless consent is obtained from the mother and father jointly, from the surviving parent if 1 is deceased, or from 1 of the minor's parents if there is only 1legal parent available to give consent. If the court considers the child to be of sufficient age to express a preference, the court shall consult a minor under 14 years of age as to a change in his or her name, and the court shall consider the minor's wishes.

(7) The name of a minor may be changed pursuant to subsection (5) or (6) with the consent or signature of the custodial parent upon notice to the non custodial parent pursuant to supreme court rule and after a hearing in either of the following circumstances: (a) If both of the following occur: (i) The other parent, having the ability to support or assist in supporting the child, has failed or neglected to provide regular

and substantial support for the child or, if a support order has been entered, has failed to substantially comply with the order, for 2 years or more before the filing of the petition. (ii) The other parent, having the ability to visit, contact, or communicate with the child, has regularly and substantially failed or neglected to do so for 2 years or more before the filing of the petition. (b) The other parent has been convicted of a violation of section 136b, 520b, 520c, 520d, 520e, or 520g of the Michigan penal code, Act No. 328 of the Public Acts of 1931, being sections 750.136b, 750.520b to 750.520e, and 750.520g of the Michigan Compiled Laws, and the child or a sibling of the child is a victim of the crime.

MINNESOTA

MINNESOTA STATUTES

259.10 General requirements. Subdivision 1. Procedure.

A person who shall have resided in this state for six months may apply to the district court in the county where the person resides to change the person's name, the names of minor children, if any, and the name of a spouse, if the spouse joins in the application, in the manner herein specified. The person shall state in the application the name and age of the spouse and each of the children, if any, and shall describe all lands in the state in or upon which the person, the children and the spouse if their names are also to be changed by the application, claim any interest or lien, and shall appear personally before the court and prove identity by at least two witnesses. If the person be a minor, the application shall be made by the person's guardian or next of kin. The court shall accept the certificate of dissolution prepared pursuant to section 518.148 as conclusive evidence of the facts recited in the certificate and may not require the person to provide the court a copy of the judgment and decree of dissolution. Every person who, with intent to defraud, shall make a false statement in any such application shall be guilty of a misdemeanor provided, however, that no minor child's name may be changed without both parents having notice of the pending of the application for change of name, whenever practicable, as determined by the court.

Subd. 2. Witness and victim protection name changes; private data. If the court determines that the name change for an individual is made in connection with the individual's participation in a witness and victim protection program, the court shall order that the court records of the name change are not accessible to the public; except that they may be released, upon request, to a law enforcement agency, probation officer, or corrections agent conducting a lawful investigation. The existence of an application for a name change described in this subdivision may not be disclosed except to a law enforcement agency conducting a lawful investigation.

259.11 Order; filing copies.

(a) Upon meeting the requirements of section 259.10, the court shall grant the application unless it finds that there is an intent to defraud or mislead or in the case of the change of a minor child's name, the court finds that such name change is not in the best interests of the child. The court shall set forth in the order the name and age of the applicant's spouse and each child of the applicant, if any, and shall state a description of the lands, if any, in which the applicant and the spouse and children, if any, claim to have an interest. The court administrator shall file such order, and record the same in the judgment book. If lands be described therein, a certified copy of the order shall be filed for record, by the applicant, with the county recorder of each county wherein any of the same are situated. Before doing so the court administrator shall present the same to the county auditor who shall enter the change of name in the auditor's official records and note upon the instrument, over an official signature, the words "change of name recorded." Any such order shall not be filed, nor any certified copy thereof be issued, until the applicant shall have paid to the county recorder and court administrator the fee required by law. No application shall be denied on the basis of the marital status of the applicant.

(b) When a person applies for a name change, the court shall determine whether the person has been convicted of a felony in this or any other state. If so, the court shall, within ten days after the name change application is granted, report the name change to the bureau of criminal apprehension. The person whose name is changed shall also report the change to the bureau of criminal apprehension within ten days. The court granting the name change application must explain this reporting duty in its order. Any person required to report the person's name change to the bureau of criminal apprehension who fails to report the name change as required under this paragraph is guilty of a gross misdemeanor.

MISSISSIPPI

§ 93-17-1. Jurisdiction to alter names and legitimate offspring; legitimation by subsequent marriage.

(1) The chancery court or the chancellor in vacation of the county of the residence of the petitioners shall have jurisdiction upon the petition of any person to alter the names of such person to make legitimate

any living offspring of the petitioner not born in wedlock and to decree said offspring to be an heir of the petitioner.

(2) An illegitimate child shall become a legitimate child of the natural father if the natural father marries the natural mother and acknowledges the child.

MISSOURI

Petition where presented—contents—proceedings.

527.270. Hereafter every person desiring to change his or her name may present a petition to that effect, verified by affidavit, to the circuit court in the county of the petitioner's residence, which petition shall set forth the petitioner's full name, the new name desired, and a concise statement of the reason for such desired change; and it shall be the duty of the judge of such court to order such change to be made, and spread upon the records of the court, in proper form, if such judge is satisfied that the desired change would be proper and not detrimental to the interests of any other person.

527.280. The fees for proceedings under sections 527.270 to 527.290 shall be the same as are now or may hereafter be allowed in similar cases in said court, to be paid by the petitioner.

Notice of change to be given, when and how.

527.290. Public notice of such a change of name shall be given at least three times in a newspaper published in the county where such person is residing, within twenty days after the order of court is made, and if no newspaper is published in his or any adjacent county, then such notice shall be given in a newspaper published in the city of St. Louis, or at the seat of government.

MONTANA

Chapter 31. CHANGE OF NAME

PART 1. GENERAL PROVISIONS

27-31-101. Petition for change of name of natural person.

All applications for change of names must be made to the district court of the county where the person whose name is proposed to be changed resides, by petition signed by such person and, if such person is under 18 years of age, by one of the parents, if living, or if both be dead, then by the guardian, and if there be no guardian, then by some near relative or friend. The petition must specify the place of birth and residence of such person, his or her present name, the name proposed, and the reason for such change of name and must, if neither parent of such person be living, name as far as known to the petitioner the near relatives of such person and their place of residence.

PART 2. PROCEDURE

27-31-201. Order setting hearing date — notice — safety.

(1) When a petition setting out the matters contained in 27-31-101 or 27-31-102 is filed, the court or judge may appoint a time for hearing the petition. Except as provided in subsections (2) and (3), notice of the time and place of hearing the petition must be published for 4 successive weeks in some newspaper published in the county, if a newspaper is printed in the county. If a newspaper is not printed in the county, a copy of the notice must be posted in at least three public places in the county for 4 successive weeks.

27-31-204. Court order.

The court or judge may make an order changing the name or dismissing the applications, as to the court or judge may seem right and proper.

NEBRASKA

61-101. Change of name; authority of district court.

The district court shall have authority to change the names of persons, towns, villages and cities within this state.

> Annotations: Whether a minor child's surname may be changed depends on, and is determined by, the best interests of the child. Factors to be considered are (1) the misconduct by one of the child's parents, (2) a parent's failure to support the child, (3) parental failure to maintain contact with the child, (4) the length of time that a surname has been used for or by the child, and (5) whether the child's surname is different from the surname of the child's custodial parent. Additionally, a court may consider the child's reasonable preference for a surname; the effect of the name change on the child's relationship with each parent; community respect associated with the surname; the difficulties, harassment, or embarrassment associated with either the present or proposed surname; and the identification of the child as part of the family unit.

61-102. Change of name; persons; procedure.

(1) Any person desiring to change his or her name may file a petition in the district court of the county in which such person may be a resident, setting forth (a) that the petitioner has been a bona fide citizen of such

county for at least one year prior to the filing of the petition, (b) the cause for which the change of petitioner's name is sought, and (c) the name asked for.

(2) Notice of the filing of the petition shall be published in a newspaper in the county, and if no newspaper is printed in the county, then in a newspaper of general circulation therein. The notice shall be published (a) once a week for four consecutive weeks if the petitioner is nineteen years of age or older at the time the action is filed and (b) once a week for two consecutive weeks if the petitioner is under nineteen years of age at the time the action is filed. In an action involving a petitioner under nineteen years of age who has a noncustodial parent, notice of the filing of the petition shall be sent by certified mail within five days after publication to the noncustodial parent at the address provided to the clerk of the district court pursuant to subsection (1) of section 42-364.13 for the noncustodial parent if he or she has provided an address. The clerk of the district court shall provide the petitioner with the address upon request.

(3) It shall be the duty of the district court, upon being duly satisfied by proof in open court of the truth of the allegations set forth in the petition, that there exists proper and reasonable cause for changing the name of the petitioner, and that notice of the filing of the petition has been given as required by this section, to order and direct a change of name of such petitioner and that an order for the purpose be made in the journals of the court.

NEVADA

PROCEEDINGS TO CHANGE NAMES OF PERSONS

NRS 41.270 Verified petition.

Any person desiring to have his name changed may file a verified petition with the clerk of the district court of the district in which he resides. The petition shall be addressed to the court and shall state the applicant's present name, the name which he desires to bear in the future, the reason for desiring the change and whether he has been convicted of a felony.

NRS 41.280 Publication of notice.

Upon the filing of the petition the applicant shall make out and procure a notice, which shall state the fact of the filing of the petition, its object, his present name and the name which he desires to bear in the future. The notice shall be published in some newspaper of general circulation in the county once a week for 3 successive weeks.

NRS 41.290 Order of court; hearing on objections; disposition and rescission of order.

1. If, within 10 days after the last publication of the notice no written objection is filed with the clerk, upon proof of the filing of the petition and publication of notice as required in NRS 41.280, and upon being satisfied by the statements in the petition, or by other evidence, that good reason exists therefor, the court shall make an order changing the name of the applicant as prayed for in the petition. If, within the period an objection is filed, the court shall appoint a day for hearing the proofs, respectively, of the applicant and the objection, upon reasonable notice. Upon that day the court shall hear the proofs, and grant or refuse the prayer of the petitioner, according to whether the proofs show satisfactory reasons for making the change. Before issuing its order, the court shall specifically take into consideration the applicant's criminal record, if any, which is stated in the petition.

2. Upon the making of an order either granting or denying the prayer of the applicant, the order must be recorded as a judgment of the court. If the petition is granted, the name of the applicant must thereupon be as stated in the order and the clerk shall transmit a certified copy of the order to the state registrar of vital statistics.

3. If an order grants a change of name to a person who has a criminal record, the clerk shall transmit a certified copy of the order to the central repository for Nevada records of criminal history for inclusion in that person's record of criminal history.

4. Upon receiving uncontrovertible proof that an applicant in his petition falsely denied having been convicted of a felony, the court shall rescind its order granting the change of name and the clerk shall transmit a certified copy of the order rescinding the previous order to:

(a) The state registrar of vital statistics for inclusion in his records.

(b) The central repository for Nevada records of criminal history for inclusion in his record of criminal history.

NEW HAMPSHIRE

TITLE 56 Probate Courts And Decedents' Estates

CHAPTER 547 Judges of Probate and Their Jurisdiction

SECTION 547:3-i Change of Name.

The probate court may grant the petition of any person to change the name of that person or the name of another person. The court shall not require the petitioner to obtain consents to the name change. The court may proceed with or without notice, in accordance with RSA 550:4.

NEW JERSEY

NEW JERSEY PERMANENT STATUTES

TITLE 2A ADMINISTRATION OF CIVIL AND CRIMINAL JUSTICE2A:52-1.

2A:52-1. Action for change of name.

Any person may institute an action in Superior Court, for authority to assume another name. The complaint for a change of name shall be accompanied by a sworn affidavit stating the applicant's name, date of birth, social security number, whether or not the applicant has ever been convicted of a crime, and whether any criminal charges are pending against him and, if such convictions or pending charges exist, shall provide such details in connection therewith sufficient to readily identify the matter referred to. The sworn affidavit shall also recite that the action for a change of name is not being instituted for purposes of avoiding or obstructing criminal prosecution or for avoiding creditors or perpetrating a criminal or civil fraud. If criminal charges are pending, the applicant shall serve a copy of the complaint and affidavit upon any State or county prosecuting authority responsible for the prosecution of any pending charges. A person commits a crime of the fourth degree if he knowingly gives or causes to be given false information under this section. Amended 1981,c.362,s.1, 1993,c.228,s.1.

NEW MEXICO

NEW MEXICO STATUTES 40-8-1.

Change of name; petition and order.

Any resident of this state over the age of fourteen years may, upon petition to the district court of the district in which the petitioner resides and upon filing the notice required with proof of publication, if no sufficient cause is shown to the contrary, have his name changed or established by order of the court. The parent or guardian of any resident of this state under the age of fourteen years may, upon petition to the district court of the district in which the petitioner resides and upon filing the notice required with proof of publication, if no sufficient cause is shown to the contrary, have the name of his child or ward changed or established by order of the court. When residents under the age of fourteen years petition the district court for a name change, the required notice shall include notice to both legal parents. The order shall be entered at length upon the record of the court, and a copy of the order, duly certified, shall be filed in the office of the county clerk of the county in which the person resides. The county clerk shall record the same in a record book to be kept by him for that purpose.

Before making application to the court for changing or establishing a name as above provided, the applicant must cause a notice thereof, stating therein the nature of the application, the time and place, when and where the same will be made, to be published in the county where such application is to be made, and where said applicant resides, said notice to be published at least once each week for two consecutive weeks, in some newspaper printed in said county, and if there be no newspaper published in the county where said applicant resides, then said notice shall be published in a newspaper printed in a county nearest to the residence of said person, and having a circulation in the county where such person resides.

That the hearing and determination of all proceedings instituted under the provisions of this chapter, and the final order of the court therein, shall be had and made at some regular term of the district court sitting within and for the county wherein said petitioner resides.

NEW YORK

NEW YORK STATE CONSOLIDATED LAWS: CIVIL RIGHTS

ARTICLE 6 CHANGE OF NAME

Sec. 60. Petition for change of name.

A petition for leave to assume another name may be made by a resident of the state to the county court of the county or the supreme court in the county in which he resides, or, if he resides in the city of New York, either to the supreme court or to any branch of the civil court of the city of New York, in any county of the city of New York. The petition to change the name of an infant may be made by the infant through his next friend, or by either of his parents, or by his general guardian, or by the guardian of his person.

Sec. 61. Contents.

The petition must be in writing, signed by the petitioner and verified in like manner as a pleading in a court of record, and must specify the grounds of the application, the name, date of birth, place of birth, age and residence of the individual whose name is proposed to be changed and the name which he proposes to assume. The petition must also specify whether or not the petitioner has been convicted of a crime or adjudicated a bankrupt, and whether or not there are any judgments or liens of record against the petitioner or actions or proceedings pending to which the petitioner is a party, and, if so, the petitioner must give descriptive details in connection therewith sufficient to readily identify the matter referred to.

Upon all applications for change of name by persons born in the state of New York, there shall be annexed to such petition either a birth certificate or a certified transcript thereof or a certificate of the commissioner or local board of health that none is available.

Sec. 62. Notice.

If the petition be to change the name of an infant, notice of the time and place when and where the petition will be presented must be served, in like manner as a notice of a motion upon an attorney in an action, upon (a) both parents of the infant, if they be living, unless the petition be made by one of the parents, in which case notice must be served upon the other, if he or she be living, and (b) the general guardian or guardian of the person, if there be one. But if any of the persons, required to be given notice by this section, reside without the state, then the notice required by this section must be sent by registered mail to the last known address of the person to be served. If it appears to the satisfaction of the court that a person required to be given notice by this section cannot be located with due diligence within the state, and that such person has no known address without the state, then the court may dispense with notice or require notice to be given to such persons and in such manner as the court thinks proper.

Sec. 63. Order.

If the court to which the petition is presented is satisfied thereby, or by the affidavit and certificate presented therewith, that the petition is true, and that there is no reasonable objection to the change of name proposed, and if the petition be to change the name of an infant, that the interests of the infant will be substantially promoted by the change, the court shall make an order authorizing the petitioner to assume the name proposed. The order shall further recite the date and place of birth of the applicant and, if the applicant was born in the state of New York, such order shall set forth the number of his birth certificate or that no birth certificate is available. The order shall be directed to be entered and the papers on which it was granted to be filed prior to the publication hereinafter directed in the clerk's office of the county in which the petitioner resides if he be an individual, or in the office of the clerk of the civil court of the city of New York if the order be made by that court. Such order shall also direct the publication, at least once, within twenty days after the making of the order, in a designated newspaper in the county in which the order is directed to be entered, of a notice in substantially the following form:

Notice is hereby given that an order entered by the........... court,........... county, on the...... day of......., bearing Index Number..........., a copy of which may be examined at the office of the clerk, located at..........., in room number......., grants me the right to assume the name of.............

My present address is....................; the date of my birth is...................; the place of my birth is....................; my present name is...........................

Sec. 64-a. Exemption from publication requirements.

If the court shall find that the publication of an applicant's change of name would jeopardize such applicant's personal safety, the provisions of sections sixty-three and sixty-four of this article requiring publication shall be waived and shall be inapplicable. The court shall order the records of such change of name proceeding to be sealed, to be opened only by order of the court for good cause shown or at the request of the applicant.

Sec. 65. Optional change of name upon marriage, divorce or annulment.

1. Any person may, upon marriage, elect to assume a new name according to the provisions of paragraph (b) of subdivision one of section fifteen of the domestic relations law.

2. Any person may, upon divorce or annulment, elect to resume the use of a former surname according to the provisions of section 240a of the domestic relations law.

3. The effect of the name changes accomplished in the manner prescribed in subdivisions one and two of this section shall be as set forth in section sixty-four of this chapter.

4. Nothing in this article shall be construed to abrogate or alter the common law right of every person, whether married or single, to retain his or her name or to assume a new one so long as the new name is used consistently and without intent to defraud.

NORTH CAROLINA

General Statutes

101-1. Legislature may regulate change by general but not private law.

The General Assembly shall not have power to pass any private law to alter the name of any person, but shall have power to pass general laws regulating the same.

101-2. Procedure for changing name; petition; notice.

A person who wishes, for good cause shown, to change his name must file his application before the clerk of the superior court of the county in which he lives, having first given 10 days' notice of the application by publication at the courthouse door. Applications to change the name of minor children may be filed by their parent or parents or guardian or next friend of such minor children, and such applications may be joined in the application for a change of name filed by their parent or parents: Provided nothing herein shall be construed to permit one parent to make such application on behalf of a minor child without the consent of the other parent of such minor child if both parents be living, except that a minor who has reached the age of 16 years, upon proper application to the clerk may change his or her name, with the consent of the a parent who has custody of the minor and has supported the minor, without the necessity of obtaining the consent of the other parent, when the clerk of court is satisfied that the other parent has abandoned the minor. Provided, further, that a change of parentage or the addition of information relating to parentage on the birth certificate of any person shall be made pursuant to G.S.130A-118. Notwithstanding any other provisions of this section, the consent of a parent who has abandoned a minor child shall not be required if there is filed with the clerk a copy of an order of a court of competent jurisdiction adjudicating that such parent has abandoned such minor child. In the event that a court of competent jurisdiction has not therefore declared the minor child to be an abandoned child then on written notice of not less than 10 days to the parent allege to have abandoned the child, by registered or certified mail directed to such parent's last known address, the clerk of superior court is hereby authorized to determine whether an abandonment has taken place. If said parent denies that an abandonment has taken place, this issue of fact shall be determined as provided in G.S. 1-273, and if abandonment is determined, then the consent of said parent shall not be required. Upon final determination of this issue of fact the proceeding shall be transferred back to the special proceedings docket for further action by the clerk.

101-3. Contents of petition.

The applicant shall state in the application his true name, county of birth, date of birth, the full name of parents as shown on birth certificate, the name he desires to adopt, his reasons for desiring such change, and whether his name has ever before been changed by law, and, if so, the facts with respect thereto.

101-4. Proof of good character to accompany petition.

The applicant shall also file with said petition proof of his good character, which proof must be made by at least two citizens of the county who know his standing: Provided, however, proof of good character shall not be required when the application is for the change of name of a child under 16 years of age.

101-5. Clerk to order change; certificate and record.

If the clerk thinks that good and sufficient reason exists for the change of name, it shall be his duty to issue an order changing the name of the applicant from his true name to the name sought to be adopted. Such order shall contain the true name, the county of birth, the date of birth, the full name of parents as shown on birth certificate, and the name sought to be adopted. He shall issue to the applicant a certificate under his hand and seal of office, stating the change made in the applicant's name, and shall also record said application and order on the docket of special proceedings in his court. He shall forward the order to the State Registrar of Vital Statistics on a form provided by him. If the applicant was born in North Carolina, the State Registrar shall note the change of name of the individual or individuals specified in the order on the birth certificate of that individual or those individuals and shall notify the register of deeds in the county of birth. If the applicant was born in another state of the United States, the State Registrar shall forward the notice of change of name to the registration office of the state of birth.

North Carolina General Statutes 101-6. Effect of change; only one change, except as provided. (a) When the order is made and the applicant's name changed, he is entitled to all the privileges and protection under his new name as he would have been under the old name. No person shall be allowed to change his name under this Chapter but once, except that he shall be permitted to resume his former name upon compliance with the requirements and procedure set forth in this Chapter for change of name, and except as provided in subsection (b) of this section. (b) For good cause shown, and upon compliance with the requirements and procedure set forth in this Chapter for change of name the name of a minor child may be changed not more than two times under this Chapter.(1891, c. 145; Rev., ss. 2147, 2149; C.S., s. 2975; 1945, c. 37,s. 2; 1991, c. 333, s. 1.)

101-8. Resumption of name by widow or widower.

A person at any time after the person is widowed may, upon application to the clerk of court of the county in which the person resides setting forth the person's intention to do so, resume the use of her maiden name or the name of a prior deceased husband or of a previously divorced husband in the case of a widow, or his pre-marriage surname in the case of a widower. The application shall set forth the full name of the last spouse of the applicant, shall include a copy of the spouse's death certificate, and shall be signed by the applicant in the applicant's full name. The clerks of court of the several counties of this State shall record and index such applications in the manner required by the Administrative Office of the Courts.

NORTH DAKOTA

Title 32 Judicial Remedies, Chapter 32-28 Change of Names of Persons and Places,

§32-28-01

1. Any person desiring to change that person's name may file a petition in the district court of the county in which the person is a resident, setting forth:

a. That the petitioner has been a bona fide resident of the county for at least six months before the filing of the petition.

b. The reason for which the change of the petitioner's name is sought.

c. The name requested.

2. The judge of the district court, upon being duly satisfied by affidavit or proof in open court of the truth of the allegations set forth in the petition, that there exists proper and reasonable cause for changing the name of the petitioner, and that thirty days' previous notice of the intended application has been given in the official newspaper of the county in which the petitioner resides, shall order a change of the name of the petitioner. The court may waive publication of the notice when the proposed change relates only to a first or given name as distinguished from a surname or upon evidence satisfactory to the court that the petitioner has been the victim of domestic violence as defined in section 14-07.1-01.

OHIO

Section 2717.01 General Assembly: 116.

Bill Number: Amended Sub. S.B. 248 Effective Date: 12-17-86

(A) A person desiring a change of name may file an application in the probate court of the county in which the person resides. The application shall set forth that the applicant has been a bona fide resident of that county for at least one year prior to the filing of the application, the cause for which the change of name is sought, and the requested new name.

Notice of the application shall be given once by publication in a newspaper of general circulation in the county at least thirty days before the hearing on the application. The notice shall set forth the court in which the application was filed, the case number, and the date and time of the hearing. Upon proof that proper notice was given and that the facts set forth in the application show reasonable and proper cause for changing the name of the applicant, the court may order the change of name.

(B) An application for change of name may be made on behalf of a minor by either of the minor's parents, a legal guardian, or a guardian ad litem. When application is made on behalf of a minor, in addition to the notice and proof required pursuant to division (A) of this section, the consent of both living, legal parents of the minor shall be filed, or notice of the hearing shall be given to the parent or parents not consenting by certified mail, return receipt requested. If there is no known father of the minor, the notice shall be given to the person who the mother of the minor alleges to be the father. If no father is so alleged, or if either parent or the address if either parent is unknown, notice pursuant to division (A) of this section shall be sufficient as to the father or parent. Any additional notice required by this division may be waived in writing by any person entitled to the notice.

OKLAHOMA

Title 12. Civil Procedure

Chapter 33 §1631. Right to Petition for Change of Name.

Any natural person, who has been domiciled in this state or who has been residing upon any military reservation located in said state, for more than thirty (30) days, and has been an actual resident of the county or such military reservation situated in said county, or county in which the military reservation is situated, for more than thirty (30) days, next preceding the filing of the action, may petition for a change of name in a civil action in the district court. If the person be a minor, the action may be brought by guardian or next friend as in other actions.

§1632. Required Context of Petition.

The petition shall be verified and shall state: (a) The name and address of the petitioner; (b) The facts as to domicile and residence; (c) The date and place of birth; (d) The birth certificate number, and place where the birth is registered, if registered; (e) The name desired by petitioner; (f) A clear and concise statement of the reasons for the desired change; (g) A positive statement that the change is not sought for any illegal or fraudulent purpose, or to delay or hinder creditors.

§1633. Notice - Protest - Hearing Date - Continuance.

Notice of filing of such petition shall be given, in the manner provided for publication notice in civil cases, by publishing the same one time at least ten (10) days prior to the date set for hearing in some newspaper authorized by law to publish legal notices printed in the county where the petition is filed if there be any printed in such county, and if there be none, then in some such newspaper printed in this state of general circulation in that county. The notice shall contain the style and number of the case, the time, date and place where the same is to be heard, and that any person may file a written protest in the case prior to the date set for the hearing. The hearing date may be any day after completion of the publication. The court or judge, for cause, may continue the matter to a later date.

OREGON

33.410 Jurisdiction; grounds.

Application for change of name of a person may be heard and determined by the probate court or, if the circuit court is not the probate court, the circuit court if its jurisdiction has been extended to include this section pursuant to ORS 3.275 of the county in which the person resides. The change of name shall be granted by the court unless the court finds that the change is not consistent with the public interest. [Amended by 1967 c.534 s.11; 1975 c.733 s.1]

33.420 Notice of application and decree; certificate; minor children.

(1) Before decreeing a change of name, except as provided in ORS 109.360, the court shall require public notice of the application to be given, that all persons may show cause why the same should not be granted. The court shall also require public notice to be given of the change after the entry of the decree.

(2) Before decreeing a change of name in the case of a minor child the court shall require that, in addition to the notice required under subsection (1) of this section, written notice be given to the parents of the child, both custodial and noncustodial, and to any legal guardian of the child. [Amended by 1983 c.369 s.6; 1997 c.872 s.22]

33.430 Name of child on birth certificate, how changed; court conference with child.

(1) In the case of a change, by court order, of the name of the parents of any minor child, if the child's birth certificate is on file in this state, the State Registrar of the Center for Health Statistics, upon receipt of a certified copy of the court order changing the name, together with the information required to locate the original birth certificate of the child, shall prepare a new birth certificate for the child in the new name of the parents of the child. The name of the parents as so changed shall be set forth in the new certificate, in place of their original name.

(2) The evidence upon which the new certificate was made, and the original certificate, shall be sealed and filed by the State Registrar of the Center for Health Statistics, and may be opened only upon demand of the person whose name was changed, if of legal age, or by an order of a court of competent jurisdiction.

(3) When a change of name by parents will affect the name of their child or children under subsection (1) of this section, the court, on its own motion or on request of a child of the parents, may take testimony from or confer with the child or children and may exclude from the conference the parents and other persons if the court finds that such action would be in the best interests of the child or children. However, the court shall permit an attorney for the parents to attend the conference, and the conference shall be reported. If the court finds that a change of name would not be in the best interests of the child, the court may provide in the order changing the name of the parents that such change of name shall not affect the child, and a new birth certificate shall not be prepared for the child.

33.440 Application by minor child; court conference.

When a minor child applies for a change of name under ORS 33.410, the court may, upon its own motion, confer with the child and may exclude from the conference the parents and other persons if the court finds that such action would be in the best interests of the child. However, the court shall permit an attorney for the child to attend the conference, and the conference shall be reported.

PENNSYLVANIA

§ 6. Change of name of individual.

(a) Petition for change of name.—Any person desiring to change his or her name shall file a petition in the court of common pleas of the county in which he or she shall reside, setting forth such desire and intention and the reason therefor, together with the residence of petitioner, and his or her residence or residences for and during five years prior thereto. Where the petitioner is a married person, the other spouse may join as a party petitioner, in which event, upon compliance with the provisions of this section, said spouse shall also be entitled to the benefits hereof. The court shall, thereupon, enter an order directing that notice be given of the filing of said petition and of the day set for the hearing thereon, which hearing shall be not less than one month or more than three months after the filing of said petition, and said notice shall be:

(1) Published in two newspapers of general circulation in said county or county contiguous thereto, one of which publications may be in the official paper for the publication of legal notices in said county.

(2) Given to any nonpetitioning parent of a child whose name may be affected by the proceedings.

(b) Court hearing and decree.—At the hearing of said petition, any person having lawful objection to the change of name may appear and be heard. If the court be satisfied after said hearing that there is no lawful objection to the granting of the prayer of said petition, a decree may be entered by said court changing the name as prayed for, if at said hearing the petitioner or petitioners shall present to the court proof of publication of said notice as required by the order, together with official searches of the proper offices of the county wherein petitioner or petitioners reside and of any other county wherein petitioner or petitioners may have resided within five years of the filing of his or her petition for change of name, or a certificate in lieu thereof given by a corporation authorized by law to make such searches, showing that there are no judgments or decrees of record or any other matter of like character against said petitioner or petitioners.

RHODE ISLAND

TITLE 33 Probate practice and procedure.

CHAPTER 33-22 Practice in Probate Courts

§ 33-22-28 Name change.

In every petition for change of name in the probate court, the judge shall grant or deny the petition without consideration of presence or absence of spousal consent.

§ 15-7-15 Decree of change of name.

If, in a petition for the adoption of a child, a change of the child's name is requested, the court, upon decreeing the adoption, may also decree the change of name and grant a certificate thereof.

SOUTH CAROLINA

Title 15 - Civil Remedies and Procedures

CHAPTER 49. CHANGE OF NAME

SECTION 15-49-10. Application for change of name.

(A) A person who desires to change his name may petition, in writing, a family court judge in the appropriate circuit, setting forth the reason for the change, his age, his place of residence and birth, and the name by which he desires to be known.

(B) A parent who desires to change the name of his minor child may petition, in writing, a family court judge in the appropriate circuit. The other parent, if there is not one then the child, must be named as a party in the action unless waived by the court. The court shall appoint a guardian ad litem to represent the child. The court shall grant the petition if it finds that it is in the best interest of the child.

SOUTH DAKOTA

CHAPTER 21-37. CHANGE OF NAME

§ 21-37-1. Circuit court power to change names - Pending proceedings and existing rights unaffected.

The circuit court shall have authority to change the names of persons, municipalities, and the name of any recorded plat or map of land situated within the limits of any municipality, as provided in this chapter. The change of names shall in no manner affect or alter any pending action or legal proceeding, nor any right, title, or interest whatsoever.

§ 21-37-3. Petition for change of name of person - Contents.

A petition for change of name of a person must be filed in the office of the clerk of courts of the county of petitioner's said residence, entitled in the circuit court for said county and stating that the petitioner has been a bona fide resident citizen of such county for at least six months prior to filing the petition; the cause for which change of petitioner's name is sought; and the name asked for.

§ 21-37-5. Hearing and order changing name of person.

At the time and place specified in the notice and upon proof in open court to the satisfaction of the judge thereof that notice of the hearing has been given as required in § 21-37-4 and that the allegations of the petition are true, and that there exists proper and reasonable cause for changing the name of the petitioner, the court or judge shall make an order directing a change of the name of the petitioner and directing that such order be entered by the clerk.

TENNESSEE

39.08 - Name Change:

a. Adult: The verified petition must comply with the statute and shall state the full legal name of the Petitioner, all prior names by which the Petitioner has been known, the place of residence of the petitioner(s), the birth date, age, social security number of the individual whose name is to be changed, and the State where the original birth certificate was issued. Copes of the original birth certificate, social security card and official photo identification shall be submitted with the petition. The individual whose name is to be changed must appear in Court at the hearing.

b. Minor: The verified petition to change the name of a minor must comply with the statute and be sworn to and signed by both parents and include copies of the original birth certificates of the child and both parents, social security card and official photo identification of both parents, photograph of the minor and social security card of the minor, if any. Both parents and the minor must appear in Court. If both parents do not join in the Petition or if the identity or location of a parent is unknown, the petition must be specific as to all pertinent facts including all efforts to identify or locate the parent who did not join in the Petition. If the father is not identified on the birth certificate, legitimation proceedings must be completed prior to filing of a petition to change the name of the minor child. Service of process is required for any parent or guardian who does not join in the petition. The verified petition must establish by clear and convincing evidence that the proposed name change is in the best interest of the minor, otherwise the petition shall not be granted.

TEXAS

FAMILY CODE - SUBTITLE C. CHANGE OF NAME

Sec. 45.102. REQUIREMENTS OF PETITION.

(a) A petition to change the name of an adult must be verified and include:

(1) the present name and place of residence of the petitioner;

(2) the full name requested for the petitioner;

(3) the reason the change in name is requested;

(4) whether the petitioner has been the subject of a final felony conviction; and

(5) whether the petitioner is subject to the registration requirements of Chapter 62, Code of Criminal Procedure.

(6) a legible and complete set of the petitioner's fingerprints on a fingerprint card format acceptable to the Department of Public Safety and the Federal Bureau of Investigation.

(b) The petition must include each of the following or a reasonable explanation why the required information is not included:

(1) the petitioner's:

(A) full name;

(B) sex;

(C) race;

(D) date of birth;

(E) driver's license number for any driver's license issued in the 10 years preceding the date of the petition;

(F) social security number; and

(G) assigned FBI number, state identification number, if known, or any other reference number in a criminal history record system that identifies the petitioner;

(2) any offense above the grade of Class C misdemeanor for which the petitioner has been charged; and

(3) the case number and the court if a warrant was issued or a charging instrument was filed or presented for an offense listed in Subsection (b)(2).

Sec. 45.002. REQUIREMENTS OF PETITION.

(a) A petition to change the name of a child must be verified and include:

(1) the present name and place of residence of the child;

(2) the reason a change of name is requested;

(3) the full name requested for the child;

(4) whether the child is subject to the continuing exclusive jurisdiction of a court under Chapter 155; and

(5) whether the child is subject to the registration requirements of Chapter 62, Code of Criminal Procedure.

(b) If the child is 10 years of age or older, the child's written consent to the change of name must be attached to the petition.

Sec. 45.003. CITATION.

(a) The following persons are entitled to citation in a suit under this subchapter:

(1) a parent of the child whose parental rights have not been terminated;

(2) any managing conservator of the child; and

(3) any guardian of the child.

(b) Citation must be issued and served in the same manner as under Chapter 102.

ORDER.

(a) The court may order the name of a child changed if:

(1) the change is in the best interest of the child; and

(2) for a child subject to the registration requirements of Chapter 62, Code of Criminal Procedure:

(A) the change is in the interest of the public; and

(B) the person petitioning on behalf of the child provides the court with proof that the child has notified the appropriate local law enforcement authority of the proposed name change.

(b) If the child is subject to the continuing jurisdiction of a court under Chapter 155, the court shall send a copy of the order to the central record file as provided in Chapter 108.

(c) In this section, "local law enforcement authority" has the meaning assigned by Article 62.01, Code of Criminal Procedure.

UTAH

42-1-1. By petition to district court — Contents.

Any natural person, desiring to change his name, may file a petition therefor in the district court of the county where he resides, setting forth:

(1) The cause for which the change of name is sought.

(2) The name proposed.

(3) That he has been a bona fide resident of the county for the year immediately prior to the filing of the petition.

42-1-2. Notice of hearing — Order of change.

The court shall order what, if any, notice shall be given of the hearing, and after the giving of such notice, if any, may order the change of name as requested, upon proof in open court of the allegations of the petition and that there exists proper cause for granting the same.

42-1-3. Effect of proceedings.

Such proceedings shall in no manner affect any legal action or proceeding then pending, or any right, title or interest whatsoever.

VERMONT

§ 811. Procedure; form

A person of age and sound mind may change his or her name by making, signing, sealing and acknowledging before the judge of the pro bate court of the district in which the person resides, an instrument in the following form:

STATE OF VERMONT }

_____ District.}

Be it remembered, that I, A. B. of _____ in the county of _____, will be hereafter known and called _____.

In witness whereof I hereunto set my hand and seal this _____ day of _____, 19 _____.

§ 812. Minor.

A minor may change his name by some person who, under chapter 111 of Title 14, may act for him, making, signing, sealing and acknowledging before the judge of the probate court of the district in which such minor resides, an instrument in substantially the form provided in section 811 of this title. Such instrument shall be signed by the person so acting for such minor. However, the name of the minor, if over fourteen years of age, shall not be changed without his consent given in court.

§ 815. Advertisement of change of name.

The court wherein an instrument changing the name is filed under this chapter shall cause notice thereof to be published for three weeks successively in a newspaper published in the county or in an adjoining county. However, such notice shall not be published when the change of name is in connection with the adoption of a minor under the age of eighteen years. The expense of a change of name and publication shall be borne by the person whose name is changed.

VIRGINIA

§ 8.01-217. How name of person may be changed.

Any person desiring to change his own name, or that of his child or ward, may apply therefor to the circuit court of the county or city in which the person whose name is to be changed resides, or if no place of abode exists, such person may apply to any circuit court which shall consider such application if it finds that good cause exists therefor under the circumstances alleged. Applications of probationers and incarcerated persons may be accepted if the court finds that good cause exists for such application. An incarcerated person may apply to the circuit court of the county or city in which such person is incarcerated. In case of a minor who has no living parent or guardian, the application may be made by his next friend. In case of a minor who has both parents living, the parent who does not join in the application shall be served with reasonable notice of the application and, should such parent object to the change of name, a hearing shall be held to determine whether the change of name is in the best interest of the minor. If, after application is made on behalf of a minor and an ex parte hearing is held thereon, the court finds by clear and convincing evidence that such notice would present a serious threat to the health and safety of the applicant, the court may waive such notice. Every application shall be under oath and shall include the place of residence of the applicant, the names of both parents, including the maiden name of his mother, the date and place of birth of the applicant, the applicant's felony conviction record, if any, whether the applicant is presently incarcerated or a probationer with any court, and if the applicant has previously changed his name, his former name or names. On any such application and hearing, if such be demanded, the court, shall, unless the evidence shows that the change of name is sought for a fraudulent purpose or would otherwise infringe upon the rights of others or, in case of a minor, that the change of name is not in the best interest of the minor, order a change of name and the clerk of the court shall spread the order upon the current deed book in his office, index it in both the old and new names, and transmit a certified copy to the State Registrar of Vital Records and the Central Criminal Records Exchange. Transmittal of a copy to the State Registrar of Vital Records and the Central Criminal Records Exchange shall not be required of a person who changed his or her former name by reason of marriage and who makes application to resume a former name pursuant to § 20-121.4. If the applicant shall show cause to believe that in the event his change of name should become a public record, a serious threat to the health or safety of the applicant or his immediate family would exist, the chief judge of the circuit court may waive the requirement that the application be under oath or the court may order the record sealed and direct the clerk not to spread and index any orders entered in the cause, and shall not transmit a certified copy to the State Registrar of Vital Records or the Central Criminal Records Exchange. Upon receipt of such order by the State Registrar of Vital Records, for a person born in this Commonwealth, together with a proper request and payment of required fees, the Registrar shall issue certifications of the amended birth record which do not reveal the former name or names of the applicant unless so ordered by a court of competent jurisdiction. Such certifications shall not be marked "amended" and show the effective date as provided in § 32.1-272. Such order shall set forth the date and place of birth of the person whose name is changed, the full names of his parents, including the maiden name of the mother and, if such person has previously changed his name, his former name or names.

WASHINGTON

(1) Any person desiring a change of his or her name or that of his or her child or ward, may apply therefor to the district court of the judicial district in which he or she resides, by petition setting forth the reasons for such change; thereupon such court in its discretion may order a change of the name and thenceforth the new name shall be in place of the former.

(2) An offender under the jurisdiction of the department of corrections who applies to change his or her name under subsection (1) of this section shall submit a copy of the application to the department of corrections not fewer than five days before the entry of an order granting the name change. No offender under the jurisdiction of the department of corrections at the time of application shall be granted an order changing his or her name if the court finds that doing so will interfere with legitimate penological interests, except that no order shall be denied

when the name change is requested for religious or legitimate cultural reasons or in recognition of marriage or dissolution of marriage. An offender under the jurisdiction of the department of corrections who receives an order changing his or her name shall submit a copy of the order to the department of corrections within five days of the entry of the order. Violation of this subsection is a misdemeanor.

(3) A sex offender subject to registration under RCW 9A.44.130 who applies to change his or her name under subsection (1) of this section shall follow the procedures set forth in *RCW 9A.44.130(6).

(4) The district court shall collect the fees authorized by RCW 36.18.010 for filing and recording a name change order, and transmit the fee and the order to the county auditor. The court may collect a reasonable fee to cover the cost of transmitting the order to the county auditor.

(5) Name change petitions may be filed and shall be heard in superior court when the person desiring a change of his or her name or that of his or her child or ward is a victim of domestic violence as defined in RCW 26.50.010(1) and the person seeks to have the name change file sealed due to reasonable fear for his or her safety or that of his or her child or ward. Upon granting the name change, the superior court shall seal the file if the court finds that the safety of the person seeking the name change or his or her child or ward warrants sealing the file. In all cases filed under this subsection, whether or not the name change petition is granted, there shall be no public access to any court record of the name change filing, proceeding, or order, unless the name change is granted but the file is not sealed. Wa. Rev. Code § 4.24.130 (2000).

WEST VIRGINIA

ARTICLE 5. CHANGE OF NAME.

§48-5-1. Petition to circuit court for change of name; contents thereof; notice of application.

Any person desiring a change of his own name, or that of his child or ward, may apply therefor to the circuit court or any other court of record having jurisdiction of the county in which he resides, or the judge thereof in vacation, by petition setting forth that he has been a bona fide resident of such county for at least one year prior to the filing of the petition, the cause for which the change of name is sought, and the new name desired; and previous to the filing of such petition such person shall cause to be published a notice of the time and place that such application will be made, which notice shall be published as a Class I legal advertisement in compliance with the provisions of article three, chapter fifty-nine of this code, and the publication area for such publication shall be the county.

§48-5-2. Objections to change of name.

Any person who is likely to be injured by the change of name of any person so petitioning, or who knows of any reason why the name of any such petitioner should not be changed, may appear at the time and place named in the notice, and shall be heard in opposition to such change.

§48-5-3. When court may order change of name.

Upon the filing of such petition, and upon proof of the publication of such notice and of the matters set forth in the petition, and being satisfied that no injury will be done to any person by reason of such change, that reasonable and proper cause exists for changing the name of petitioner, and that such change is not desired because of any fraudulent or evil intent on the part of the petitioner, the court or judge thereof in vacation may order a change of name as applied for except as provided by the provisions of this section. The court may not grant any change of name for any person convicted of any felony during the time that the person is incarcerated. The court may not grant any change of name for any person required to register with the state police pursuant to the provisions of article eight-f, chapter sixty-one of this code during the period that such person is required to register. The court may not grant a change of name for persons convicted of first degree murder in violation of section one, article two, chapter sixty-one of this code for a period of ten years after the person is discharged from imprisonment or is discharged from parole, whichever occurs later. The court may not grant a change of name of any person convicted of violating any provision of section fourteen-a, article two, chapter sixty-one of this code for a period of ten years after the person is discharged from imprisonment or is discharged from parole, whichever occurs later.

§48-5-4. Recordation of order changing name.

When such order is made the petitioner shall forthwith cause a certified copy thereof to be filed in the office of the clerk of the county court of the county where petitioner resides, and such clerk shall record the same in a book to be kept for the purpose and index the same under both the old and the new names. For such recording and indexing the clerk shall be allowed the same fee as for a deed.

§48-5-5. When new name to be used.

When such change has been ordered and a certified copy of the order filed in the office of the county clerk, the new name shall thenceforth be used in place of the former name.

§48-5-6. Unlawful change of name.

Any person residing in this state who shall change his name, or assume another name, unlawfully, shall be guilty of a misdemeanor, and, upon conviction thereof, shall be fined not exceeding one hundred dollars, and upon a repetition thereof shall be confined in jail not exceeding sixty days.

§48-5-7. Unlawful change of name by certain felons and registrants.

(a) It is unlawful for any person convicted of first degree murder in violation of section one, article two, chapter sixty-one of this code, and for any person convicted of violating any provision of section fourteen-a, article two, chapter sixty-one of this code, for which a sentence of life imprisonment is imposed, to apply for a change of name for a period of ten years after the person is discharged from imprisonment or is discharged from parole, whichever occurs later.

(b) It is unlawful for any person required to register with the state police pursuant to the provisions of article twelve, chapter fifteen of this code to apply for a change of name during the period that the person is required to register.

(c) It is unlawful for any person convicted of a felony to apply for a change of name during the period that such person is incarcerated.

(d) A person who violates the provisions of subsections (a), (b) or (c) of this section is guilty of a misdemeanor and, upon conviction thereof, shall be fined not less than two hundred fifty dollars nor more than ten thousand dollars or imprisoned in the county or regional jail for not more than one year, or both fined and incarcerated.

WISCONSIN

786.36 Changing names, court procedure.

Any resident of this state, whether a minor or adult, may upon petition to the circuit court of the county where he or she resides and upon filing a copy of the notice, with proof of publication, as required by § 786.37, if no sufficient cause is shown to the contrary, have his or her name changed or established by order of the court. If the person whose name is to be changed is a minor under the age of 14 years, the petition may be made by: both parents, if living, or the survivor of them; the guardian or person having legal custody of the minor if both parents are dead or if the parental rights have been terminated by judicial proceedings; or the mother, if the minor is a nonmarital child who is not adopted or whose parents do not subsequently intermarry under § 767.60, except that the father must also make the petition unless his rights have been legally terminated. The order shall be entered at length upon the records of the court and a certified copy of the record shall be recorded in the office of the register of deeds of the county, who shall make an entry in a book to be kept by the register. The fee for recording a certified copy is the fee specified under § 59.43 (2) (ag). If the person whose name is changed or established was born or married in this state, the clerk of the court shall send to the state registrar of vital statistics, on a form designed by the state registrar of vital statistics, an abstract of the record, duly certified, accompanied by the fee prescribed in § 69.22, which fee the clerk of court shall charge to and collect from the petitioner. The state registrar of vital statistics shall then correct the birth record, marriage record or both, and direct the register of deeds and local registrar to make similar corrections on their records. No person engaged in the practice of any profession for which a license is required by the state may change his or her given name or his or her surname to any other given name or any other surname than that under which the person was originally licensed in the profession in this or any other state, in any instance in which the state board or commission for the particular profession, after a hearing, finds that practicing under the changed name operates to unfairly compete with another practitioner or misleads the public as to identity or otherwise results in detriment to the profession or the public. This prohibition against a change of name by a person engaged in the practice of any profession does not apply to any person legally qualified to teach in the public schools in this state, nor to a change of name resulting from marriage or divorce, nor to members of any profession for which there exists no state board or commission authorized to issue licenses or pass upon the qualifications of applicants or hear complaints respecting conduct of members of the profession. Any change of name other than as authorized by law is void.

WYOMING

CHAPTER 25 CHANGE OF NAME

1-25-101. Verified petition to be presented; information to be shown in petition; order of court making change; record to be made.

Every person desiring to change his name may petition the district court of the county of the petitioner's residence for the desired change. The petition shall be verified by affidavit setting forth the petitioner's full name, the name desired, a concise statement of the reason for the desired change, the place of his birth, his place of residence and the length of time he has been an actual bona fide resident of the county in which the petition is filed. If the court is satisfied that the desired change is proper and not detrimental to the interests of any other person, it shall order the change to be made, and record the proceedings in the records of the court.

1-25-102. Residence requirement.

A person petitioning for a change of name shall have been a bona fide resident of the county in which the petition is filed for at least two (2) years immediately preceding filing the petition.

1-25-103. Notice to be given by publication.

Public notice of the petition for a change of name shall be given in the same manner as service by publication upon nonresidents in civil actions.

1-25-104. Change of name in adoption proceedings.

In all cases of the adoption of children in the manner provided by law, the court before which such adoption proceeding is held, may change the name of any child so adopted and make an order to that effect, which shall be recorded in the records of the proceeding of adoption. Each child who has heretofore, in Wyoming, been adopted according to law, may have his or her name changed to that of the parents who have adopted him or her, upon the parents, who have adopted such child, on behalf of such child, filing a petition therefor.

APPENDIX 2:
SAMPLE NAME CHANGE
PETITION—ADULT

Civil Court of the City of New York

County of _____   Index Number _____

In the Matter of the Application of

                                        PETITION FOR
                                        INDIVIDUAL ADULT

for Leave to Change His/Her Name To   **CHANGE OF NAME**

_____

1.   _____ by this petition, alleges

2.   My present name is: _____.

3.   The name which I propose to assume in place and stead of my present name is:

       _____.

4.   My Age, Date of Birth and Place of Birth are: Age: _____ Date of Birth: _____

       Place of Birth: _____,

Note: *If you were born in the* <u>State of New York</u> *you must attach either: a) a Birth Certificate, b) a Certified Transcript of such Birth Certificate, or c) a Certificate from the Commissioner or the local Board of Health that no such Certificate is available.*

5.   My present residence is: _____

6.   For each of the following four questions, place your *initials* in the appropriate column.

                                                                    YES   NO

       a) Have you ever been convicted of a crime?... _____   _____

       b) Have you ever been adjudicated a bankrupt?.. _____   _____

       c) Are there judgments or liens of record against you?................................ _____   _____

       d) Are there any actions or proceedings pending to which you are a party?................... _____   _____

       If your answer is "YES" to any of the four questions above, give particulars below in sufficient detail to readily identify the matter referred to:

       _____

       _____

       _____

       _____

       (If additional space is required, attach (a) separate sheet(s) of paper with the details.)

CIV-GP-82A Page 1 (Revised October, 2003)

PETITION FOR INDIVIDUAL ADULT CHANGE OF NAME - PAGE 2

7.   I have/have not made a previous application to change my name in this or any other Court.

    (Strike out one)   *(If you have, give details and reason for this current application below.)*

_____

_____

_____

_____

8.   The reasons for this application are as follows: _____

_____

_____

9.   WHEREFORE, your Petitioner respectfully requests that an Order be granted permitting this change of name.

_____   _____
        Date   Signature of Petitioner

VERIFICATION

State of New York, County of _____ ss.:

_____, being duly sworn, deposes and says:

s/he is the petitioner named above, that petitioner has read the petition and knows the truth of the contents thereof except for those matters alleged to be on information and belief, and as to those matters, petitioner believes them to be true.

_____
                       Signature of Petitioner

Sworn to before me this _____ day of _____, 20____

_____
Signature of Notary Public

CIV-GP-82A page 2(Revised October, 2003)

APPENDIX 3:
SAMPLE NAME CHANGE PACKET WITH INSTRUCTIONS—ADULT

INSTRUCTIONS FOR CHANGE OF NAME OF AN ADULT
Instructions for Completing Dom Rel 60

Introduction:

> You must be an adult to use this form (age 18 or older). Do **not** use this form if you are filing to have a child's name changed. Use DOM REL 62 instead.
> You must be a resident of the County in which you are filing for a name change.
> You may not use these forms to change a name in connection with an adoption or a divorce.
> For more information, read Maryland Rule 15-901.

General:

> To change your name you must file a Petition for Change of Name. A notice of the request must be published in a newspaper of general circulation in the county in which you reside unless the Court grants a waiver of publication. You will need to check with the Clerk of Court regarding publication of the Notice. In some jurisdictions publication arrangements are the responsibility of the party asking for publication. In other jurisdictions the Clerk of Court will arrange to have the Notice published. After the notice has been published, other persons are given the opportunity to object. If someone objects, that person must file an objection and send a copy of the objection to you. You will have 15 days to respond to the objection by filing a written response with the Court. If you want the court to hold a hearing on the objection, include a Request for Hearing or Proceeding, DOM REL 59, with your response.

Instructions:

> STEP 1 — Completion of the Petition for Change of Name (Adult), Notice for Publication and Order for Change of Name

> A. Fill out the Petition for Change of Name, as indicated.
> B. Sign the Petition.
> C. Fill out the top section and first paragraph of the Notice for Publication. Leave the second paragraph blank.
> D. Fill out the Order for Change of Name, except for the date and Judge's signature.

>STEP 2 — Attachment of Birth Certificate

> Attach to the documents to be filed with the court, a copy of your birth certificate or other document reflecting your *current name* (the one you want to change *from*).

Page 1 of 2   DRIN 60 - Revised 15 May 2003

>STEP 3 — Filing of Documents

File the above documents with the Clerk of the court at the circuit court for the county in which you reside. Pay the filing fee. You will need to check with the Clerk of Court regarding publication of the Notice. In some jurisdictions publication arrangements are the responsibility of the party asking for publication. In other jurisdictions the Clerk of Court will arrange to have the Notice published.

>STEP 4 — Pay for the Publication of the Notice

The newspaper will send you an invoice to have the Notice published. You are required to pay this invoice. Publication can be expensive. After the Notice has been published you and the Clerk will be sent a confirmation from the newspaper.

>STEP 5 — Consideration of Petition and Issuance of Order

After the Clerk receives the confirmation from the newspaper, they will send your Petition to a judge. The judge will review all of the information.

If someone has contested the name change or if the judge has any questions about your petition, then a hearing may be scheduled. (Remember to respond to any objection within 15 days after you receive it and include a Request for Hearing or Proceeding, DOM REL 59, if you want the court to hold a hearing on the objection).

If no one has contested the change, and everything has been done properly, then the judge may sign the Order for Name Change. You will receive a certified copy of the Order in the mail, and, for a small fee, you may obtain additional certified copies of the Order from the Clerk. You will need to use a certified copy of the Order for Name Change to change your name at the Motor Vehicle Administration (you may need other identification for this), the Bureau of Vital Statistics, Social Security Administration, creditors, etc.

Page 2 of 2   DRIN 60 - Revised 15 May 2003

Circuit Court for _____
City or County

CIVIL–DOMESTIC CASE INFORMATION REPORT

Directions:

Plaintiff: This Information Report must be completed and attached to the complaint filed with the Clerk of Court unless your case is exempted from the requirement by the Chief Judge of the Court of Appeals pursuant to Rule 2-111. A copy must be included for each defendant to be served.

Defendant: You must file an Information Report as required by Rule 2-323(h).

THIS INFORMATION REPORT CANNOT BE ACCEPTED AS AN ANSWER OR RESPONSE.

FORM FILED BY: ☐ PLAINTIFF ☐ DEFENDANT CASE NUMBER:_____
(Clerk to insert)

CASE NAME: _____ v _____
Plaintiff   Defendant

PARTY'S NAME:_____ PHONE: (___)_____
(Daytime phone)

ADDRESS: _____

PARTY'S ATTORNEY'S NAME: _____ PHONE: (___)_____

ATTORNEY'S ADDRESS: _____

☐ I am not represented by an attorney

RELATED CASE PENDING? ☐ Yes ☐ No If yes, Court and Case #(s), if known _____

Special Requirements? ☐ Interpreter/communication impairment   Which language_____

(Attach Form 1-332 if Accommodation or Interpreter Needed)   Which dialect_____

☐ ADA accommodation:_____

ALTERNATIVE DISPUTE RESOLUTION INFORMATION

Is this case appropriate for referral to an ADR process under Md. Rule 17-101? (Check all that apply)

A. Mediation ☐ Yes ☐ No	C. Settlement Conference ☐ Yes ☐ No	
B. Arbitration ☐ Yes ☐ No	D. Neutral Evaluation ☐ Yes ☐ No	

IS THIS CASE CONTESTED? ☐ Yes ☐ No If yes, which issues appear to be contested?

   ☐ Ground for divorce

   ☐ Child Custody   ☐ Visitation

   ☐ Child Support

   ☐ Alimony   ☐ Permanent   ☐ Rehabilitative

   ☐ Use and possession of family home and property

   ☐ Marital property issues involving:

      ☐ Valuation of business ☐ Pensions ☐ Bank accounts/IRA's   ☐ Real Property

      ☐ Other: _____

   ☐ Paternity

   ☐ Adoption/termination of parental rights

   ☐ Other: _____

Request is made for: ☐ Initial order ☐ Modification ☐ Contempt ☐ Absolute Divorce ☐ Limited Divorce

For non-custody/visitation issues, do you intend to request:

   ☐ Court-appointed expert (name field)_____ ☐ Mediation by a Court-sponsored settlement program

   ☐ Initial conference with the Court   ☐ Other:

For custody/visitation issues, do you intend to request:

   ☐ Mediation by a private mediator   ☐ Appointment of counsel to represent child (not just to

   ☐ Evaluation by mental health professional   waive psychiatric privilege)

   ☐ Other Evaluation _____   ☐ A conference with the Court

Is there an allegation of physical or sexual abuse of party or child? ☐ Yes ☐ No

Page 1 of 2   Effective January 1, 2003

CASE NAME: _____ V _____ CASE NUMBER: _____
            Plaintiff   Defendant   (Clerk to insert)

TIME ESTIMATE FOR A MERITS HEARING: _____ hours _____ days

TIME ESTIMATE FOR HEARING OTHER THAN A MERITS HEARING: _____ hours _____ days

_____ _____
Signature of Counsel/Party   Date

_____
Print Name

_____
Street Address

_____
City/State/ZIP

Page 2 of 2   Effective January 1, 2003

IN THE MATTER OF: *   IN THE

_____ *   CIRCUIT COURT
(your current name)

_____ *   FOR
(street address)

_____ *
(city, state, zip)   _____

_____ *
(phone number)

FOR CHANGE OF NAME TO: *   Civil No.:_____

                                        *

_____
(new name)

*   *   *   *   *   *   *   *   *   *   *   *   *

PETITION FOR CHANGE OF NAME
(Adult)
(DOM REL 60)

TO THE HONORABLE, THE JUDGE OF SAID COURT:

     Petitioner, ____ _____ , respectfully represents
                               (your current name)
to this Court:

     1. That I was born on ____ _____ , in _____ ,
                         (your birthdate)   (your birthplace - city, state, country)
and presently reside at _____ .
                               (present address)
     2. That I was born ___ _____ , (See copy of
                              (your birth name)
attached birth certificate),

     [   ]   My name has been changed to the following since birth for the following reasons
           (*List any reasons why your name may have changed since birth, for example,*
           marriage).

                      Name Changed To: Reason:

                _____   _____
                _____   _____
                _____   _____
                _____   _____

     [   ]   I have attached any documents that changed my name officially.

                                     Page 1 of 2   DR 60 - Revised 13 February 2001

3. I am requesting this change of name because:

4. I wish to change my name to :_____ .
                                (new name)

5. I hereby certify that the above change of name is not requested for any illegal or fraudulent purposes.

    WHEREFORE, I respectfully request that the Court pass an Order changing my name from _____ to _____ .
          (current name)   (new name)

I, _____ , solemnly affirm under the penalties
                (your current name)

of perjury, that the contents of the foregoing paper are true to the best of my knowledge, information and belief.

_____   _____
(Date)   (Your Signature)

                                             _____
                                             (Your Name - Printed)

                                             _____
                                             (Address)

                                             _____
                                             (City, State, Zip)

                                             _____
                                             (Telephone Number)

Page 2 of 2   DR 60 - Revised 13 February 2001

IN THE MATTER OF: *   IN THE

_____   *   CIRCUIT COURT
(your current name)
                                       *   FOR
FOR CHANGE OF NAME TO:
                                       *   _____

_____   *   Civil No.:_____
(new name)

*   *   *   *   *   *   *   *   *   *   *   *   *

NOTICE
(Adult)
(DOM REL 61)

        The above Petitioner has filed a Petition for Change of Name in which he/she seeks to
change his/her name from ____ _____ _____ to
                              (your current legal name)
_____ _____ . The petitioner is seeking a name change
              (name you want)
because:

        Any person may file an objection to the Petition on or before the _____ day of

_____ _____ , _____ . The objection must be supported by an

affidavit and served upon the Petitioner in accordance with Maryland Rule 1-321. Failure to file

an objection or affidavit within the time allowed may result in a judgment by default or the

granting of the relief sought.

        A copy of this notice shall be published one time in a newspaper of general circulation in

the county/city at least fifteen (15) days before the deadline to file an objection.

                              _____
                                        CLERK

                Page 1 of 1   DR 61 - Revised 4 February 2002

Circuit Court for_____ **Case No.**_____
City or County

Name _____   Name _____

Street Address _____ Apt. # _____ **VS.** Street Address _____ Apt. # _____

City _____ State Zip Code ___ Area Telephone _____   City _____ State Zip Code ___ Area Telephone _____
Code   Code

Plaintiff   *Defendant*

CERTIFICATE OF PUBLICATION
(DOM REL 75)

I HEREBY CERTIFY that I caused the publication of the attached notice one time in the

following newspaper of general circulation: _____.
Name of Newspaper

The notice was published on _____, more than 15 days prior to the date

specified in the notice for filing an objection to the Petition for Name Change.

Date _____   Signature _____

Attach Notice Here

Page 1 of 1

DR75 - Revised 6 May 2002

IN THE MATTER OF   *   IN THE

_____   *   CIRCUIT COURT

(your current name)   *   FOR

FOR CHANGE OF NAME TO   *

    *   _____

_____   *

(new name)   *   Civil No.:_____

*   *   *   *   *   *   *   *   *   *   *   *   *

ORDER FOR CHANGE OF NAME

1. BASIS

The provisions of this order are based upon

[　] An evidentiary hearing before a [　] Judge　[　] Master.

[　] A ruling by the court without a hearing.

2. ORDER

UPON CONSIDERATION of the Petition to Change Name filed in this matter, it is hereby

ORDERED that the name of _____ be and the same is

changed to: _____

_____

JUDGE

Page 1 of 1   JO 12 - Revised 2 November 2000

APPENDIX 4:
SAMPLE NAME CHANGE PETITION—CHILD

Civil Court of the City of New York
County of _____

Index Number _____

In the Matter of the Application of

**PETITION FOR
INDIVIDUAL MINOR'S
CHANGE OF NAME**

As Parent and Natural Guardian for leave
to Change Minor's Name To

_____

1. _____, by this petition, alleges

2. I am the _____ of a Minor

3. The Minor's present name is _____.

4. The name which I propose that the Minor will assume in place and stead of the Minor's present name is:

    _____.

5. The Minor's Age, Date of Birth and Place of Birth are: Age:_____ Date of Birth:_____

    Place of Birth: _____.

    Note: If the Minor was born in the State of New York you must attach either: a) a Birth Certificate, b) a Certified Transcript of such Birth Certificate, or c) a Certificate from the Commissioner or the local Board of Health that no such Certificate is available.

6. The Minor's present residence is: _____

7. For each of the following four questions, place your *initials* in the appropriate column.

	YES	NO
a) Has the Minor ever been convicted of a crime?...	_____	_____
b) Has the Minor ever been adjudicated a bankrupt?...	_____	_____
c) Are there judgments or liens of record against the Minor?...	_____	_____
d) Are there any actions or proceedings pending to which the Minor is a party?...............	_____	_____

    If your answer is "YES" to any of the four questions above, give particulars below in sufficient detail to readily identify the matter referred to:

    _____

    _____

    _____

    (If additional space is required, attach (a) separate sheet(s) of paper with the details.)
    CIV-GP-82M Page 1 (Revised October, 2003)

PETITION FOR INDIVIDUAL MINOR'S CHANGE OF NAME - PAGE 2

6.   I have/have not made a previous application to change the Minor's name in this or any other Court.
      (Strike out one)   (If you have, give details and reason for this current application below.)

      _____

      _____

      _____

      _____

7.   The reasons for this application are as follows: _____

      _____

      _____

8.   WHEREFORE, your Petitioner respectfully requests that an Order be granted permitting this change of
      name.

      _____   _____
                 Date   Signature of Petitioner

VERIFICATION

State of New York, County of _____ ss.:

_____, being duly sworn, deposes and says:
s/he is the petitioner named above, that petitioner has read the petition and knows the truth of the contents thereof
except for those matters alleged to be on information and belief, and as to those matters, petitioner believes them to
be true.

                                            _____
                                                    Signature of Petitioner

Sworn to before me this _____ day of _____, 20___

_____
Signature of Notary Public

_____

CIV-GP-82M Page 2 (Revised October, 2003)

APPENDIX 5:
SAMPLE NAME CHANGE PACKET WITH INSTRUCTIONS—CHILD

INSTRUCTIONS FOR CHANGE OF NAME OF A MINOR
Instructions for Completing DOM REL 62

Introduction:

The minor must be a resident of the County in which you are filing for a name change. You may not use these forms to change a name in connection with an adoption. For more information, read Maryland Rule 15-901.

NOTE: *Changing the name of a child will not change an existing child support obligation.*

General:

Child Less Than 1 Year Old: If the child is less than one-year old, you may be able to change the child's name without a court order. Read MD. HEALTH GEN. CODE ANN. § 4-214.

Child Aged 1 Year or Older: To change a child's name you, as his/her parent or guardian, may file a Petition for Change of Name. Ordinarily the court will look at whether all parents, guardians and custodians, as well as the child, are in agreement with the name change. The request to have the name changed must also be published in a newspaper of general circulation in the county in which you are filing the Petition. You will need to check with the Clerk of Court regarding publication of the Notice. In some jurisdictions publication arrangements are the responsibility of the party asking for publication. In other jurisdictions the Clerk of Court will arrange to have the Notice published. After the notice has been published, other persons are given the opportunity to object. If someone objects, they must file this objection and serve you a copy. You will have 15 days to respond to the objection by filing a written response with the Court.

Instructions:

> STEP 1 — Securing Consent of Parents, Guardians or Custodians

It is usually preferable to submit the Petition with signed consents from all parents, guardians and custodians. Before preparing the Petition for Change of Name, contact each parent, guardian, or custodian. Ask that person to sign a Consent form. File this consent form with your petition.

> STEP 2 — Completion of the Petition for Change of Name (Minor), Notice and Order for Change of Name

A. Fill out the Petition for Change of Name, as indicated.

DRIN 62 - Revised 15 May 2003

B. Sign the Petition.

C. Fill out the top section and first paragraph of the Notice for Publication. Leave the second paragraph blank.

D. Fill out the proposed Order for Change of Name, except for the date and Judge's signature.

>STEP 3 — Attachment of Consent Forms and Birth Certificate

Attach to the documents to be filed with the court, each signed consent, and a copy of the child's birth certificate or other document reflecting the child's *current name* (the one you want it changed *from*).

>STEP 4 — Filing of Documents

File the above documents with the Clerk of the court at the circuit court for the county in which you reside. Pay the filing fee. You will need to check with the Clerk of Court regarding publication of the Notice. In some jurisdictions publication arrangements are the responsibility of the party asking for publication. In other jurisdictions the Clerk of Court will arrange to have the Notice published.

> STEP 5 — Service

If you have not obtained the consent of each parent, guardian and custodian of the child, you will need to serve each person who has not consented with the following papers which you have filed or which have been provided by the Court. *See **General Instructions**.*

1. Petition for Change of Name
2. Notice
3. Order for Change of Name
4. All attachments you filed with these documents
5. Writ of Summons (This will be given to you after you file your documents)

>STEP 6 — Pay for the Publication of the Notice

The newspaper will send you an invoice to have the Notice published. You are required to pay this invoice. Publication can be expensive. After the Notice has been published, you and the Clerk will be sent a confirmation from the newspaper.

>STEP 7 — Consideration of Petition and Issuance of Order

After the Clerk receives the confirmation from the newspaper, they will send your Petition to a judge. The judge will review all of the information.

DRIN 62 - Revised 15 May 2003

How to Change Your Name

If someone has contested the name change, if you have not secured the consent of all parents, guardians or custodians, or if the judge has any questions about your petition, a hearing may be scheduled. (Remember to Respond to any objection within 15 days after you receive it and include a Request for Hearing or Proceeding, DOM REL 59, if you want the court to hold a hearing on the objection).

If no one has contested the change, and everything has been done properly, then the judge may sign the proposed Order for Name Change. You will receive a certified copy of the signed Order in the mail, and, for a small fee, you may obtain additional certified copies of the Order from the Clerk. You will need to use a certified copy of the Order for Name Change to change the child's name at the Motor Vehicle Administration (you may need other identification for this), the Bureau of Vital Statistics, the Social Security Administration, with creditors, or at the child's school.

Page 3 of 3   DRIN 62 - Revised 15 May 2003

Circuit Court for _____
City or County

CIVIL–DOMESTIC CASE INFORMATION REPORT

Directions:

    Plaintiff: This Information Report must be completed and attached to the complaint filed with the Clerk of Court unless your case is exempted from the requirement by the Chief Judge of the Court of Appeals pursuant to Rule 2-111. A copy must be included for each defendant to be served.

    Defendant: You must file an Information Report as required by Rule 2-323(h).

    THIS INFORMATION REPORT CANNOT BE ACCEPTED AS AN ANSWER OR RESPONSE.

FORM FILED BY: ❏ PLAINTIFF   ❏ DEFENDANT   CASE NUMBER: _____
(Clerk to insert)

CASE NAME: _____ v _____
Plaintiff   Defendant

PARTY'S NAME: _____ PHONE: (___)_____
(Daytime phone)

ADDRESS: _____

PARTY'S ATTORNEY'S NAME: _____ PHONE: (___)_____

ATTORNEY'S ADDRESS: _____

     ❏ I am not represented by an attorney

RELATED CASE PENDING? ❏ Yes   ❏ No   If yes, Court and Case #(s), if known _____

Special Requirements? ❏ Interpreter/communication impairment   Which language_____

(Attach Form 1-332 if Accommodation or Interpreter Needed)   Which dialect_____

     ❏ ADA accommodation:_____

ALTERNATIVE DISPUTE RESOLUTION INFORMATION

Is this case appropriate for referral to an ADR process under Md. Rule 17-101? (Check all that apply)

     A. Mediation   ❏ Yes ❏ No   C. Settlement Conference ❏ Yes ❏ No

     B. Arbitration   ❏ Yes ❏ No   D. Neutral Evaluation   ❏ Yes ❏ No

IS THIS CASE CONTESTED?   ❏ Yes ❏ No   If yes, which issues appear to be contested?

     ❏ Ground for divorce

     ❏ Child Custody   ❏ Visitation

     ❏ Child Support

     ❏ Alimony   ❏ Permanent   ❏ Rehabilitative

     ❏ Use and possession of family home and property

     ❏ Marital property issues involving:

         ❏ Valuation of business   ❏ Pensions   ❏ Bank accounts/IRA's   ❏ Real Property

         ❏ Other: _____

     ❏ Paternity

     ❏ Adoption/termination of parental rights

     ❏ Other: _____

Request is made for: ❏ Initial order ❏ Modification ❏ Contempt ❏ Absolute Divorce ❏ Limited Divorce

For non-custody/visitation issues, do you intend to request:

     ❏ Court-appointed expert (name field)_____ ❏ Mediation by a Court-sponsored settlement program

     ❏ Initial conference with the Court   ❏ Other: _____

For custody/visitation issues, do you intend to request:

     ❏ Mediation by a private mediator   ❏ Appointment of counsel to represent child (not just to

     ❏ Evaluation by mental health professional   waive psychiatric privilege)

     ❏ Other Evaluation _____   ❏ A conference with the Court

Is there an allegation of physical or sexual abuse of party or child?   ❏ Yes ❏ No

Page 1 of 2   Effective January 1, 2003

CASE NAME: _____ V _____ CASE NUMBER: _____
Plaintiff   Defendant   (Clerk to insert)

TIME ESTIMATE FOR A MERITS HEARING: _____ hours _____ days

TIME ESTIMATE FOR HEARING OTHER THAN A MERITS HEARING: _____ hours _____ days

_____
Signature of Counsel/Party

_____
Date

_____
Print Name

_____
Street Address

_____
City/State/ZIP

Page 2 of 2   Effective January 1, 2003

IN THE MATTER OF: *   IN THE

_____   *   CIRCUIT COURT
(child's current name)
_____   *   FOR
(street address)
_____   *   _____
(city, state, zip)
_____   *
(phone number)
                                           *
FOR CHANGE OF NAME TO:
                                           *
_____   *
(child's new name)

BY AND THROUGH HIS/HER   *   Civil No.:_____
MOTHER/FATHER/GUARDIAN:
                                           *
_____
(petitioner's name)
*   *   *   *   *   *   *   *   *   *   *   *   *

PETITION FOR CHANGE OF NAME
(Minor)
(DOM REL 62)

TO THE HONORABLE, THE JUDGE OF SAID COURT:

Petitioner, _____ , a minor, by and through
                          (child's current name)
his/her   Mother /   Father /   Guardian (*check one*) respectfully represents to this Court:

1. That the minor child was born on _____ , in _____ ,
                                       (child's birthdate)   (child's birthplace - city, state, country)
and presently resides at _____ .
                                        (child's present address)
2. That the child's birthname is _____ .
                                        (child's birth name)

[   ]   The child's name has been changed to the following since birth for the following
        reasons (*List any reasons why the child's name may have been changed since
        birth, for example, adoption*).

                Name Changed To: Reason:

        _____   _____
        _____   _____
        _____   _____

                    Page 1 of 3   DR 62 - Revised 13 February 2001

[ ]   I have attached a birth certificate or other document reflecting the child's current name

3. Petitioner wishes to change the child's name to :_____ .

(child's new name)

4. This change of name is being requested because:

5. The name and address of each parent, guardian and custodian of the child is:

6. The other parent, guardian or custodian:

    [ ]   Consents to and joins this petition.

    [ ]   Has not consented at this time.

    [ ]   Cannot be found, and I have attached an Affidavit and Motion to Serve by Alternative Means.

7. Petitioner hereby certifies that the above change of name is not requested for any illegal or fraudulent purposes.

WHEREFORE, I respectfully request that the Court pass an Order changing the minor child's name from _____ to _____ .

(current name)   (new name)

Page 2 of 3

DR 62 - Revised 13 February 2001

I, _____ , solemnly affirm under the penalties
(your current name - MOTHER/FATHER/GUARDIAN)

of perjury, that the contents of the foregoing paper are true to the best of my knowledge,

information and belief.

_____
(Date)

_____
(Your Signature -- MOTHER/FATHER/GUARDIAN)

_____
(Your Name - Printed)

_____
(Address)

_____
(City, State, Zip)

_____
(Telephone Number)

Page 3 of 3   DR 62 - Revised 13 February 2001

IN THE MATTER OF:

_____
(child's current name)

FOR CHANGE OF NAME TO:

_____
(child's new name)

BY AND THROUGH HIS/HER
MOTHER/FATHER/GUARDIAN:

_____
(petitioner's name)

*   *   *   *   *   *

*   IN THE
*   CIRCUIT COURT
*
*   FOR
*
*   _____
*
*   Civil No.:_____
*
*

*   *   *   *   *   *

CONSENT TO CHANGE OF NAME
(Consent of Parent, Guardian or Custodian)
(DOM REL 63)

1. Name, Age and Competence.

My name is _____ . My date of birth is _ _____
and I am capable of understanding what this consent means.

2. Status as Parent or Guardian.

I am [   ] the mother [   ] the father (or) [   ] the guardian of _____ _____
(current name of child)

_____ ____ , born on _____ , _____ .
(date of birth)

3. Consent.

I hereby consent that the minor child's name be changed from _____ _____
(current name of child)
_____ _____ _ to _____ _____ . I hereby join in the foregoing
Petition and waive notice of process. I acknowledge that I have the right to revoke my consent at
any time prior to the date an order changing the child's name is entered. I acknowledge that I
was provided the opportunity to consult with legal counsel, if I so chose, before signing this
Consent.

I SOLEMNLY AFFIRM under the penalties of perjury that the contents of the foregoing
Consent are true to the best of my knowledge, information, and belief.

_____   _____
(date)   (your signature)

                       _____
                       (your name - PRINTED)

                       _____
                       (street address)

                       _____
                       (city , state , zip code)

                       _____
                       (telephone number)

NOTE: Changing the name of a child will not change an existing child support obligation.

Page 1 of 1

DR 63 - Revised 13 Feb 2001

IN THE MATTER OF: *   IN THE

_____   *   CIRCUIT COURT
(child's current name)

FOR CHANGE OF NAME TO: *   FOR

                                            *

_____   *   _____
(child's new name)

BY AND THROUGH HIS/HER   *   Civil No.:_____
MOTHER/FATHER/GUARDIAN:

_____   *
(petitioner's name)

*   *   *   *   *   *   *   *   *   *   *   *

CONSENT TO CHANGE OF NAME
(Consent of Person Originally Listed on Birth Certificate)

(DOM REL 64)

1. Name, Age and Competence.

My name is _____ . My date of birth is _____
and I am capable of understanding what this consent means.

2. Status.

I believe that I am NOT the father of _____ ,
                                                                   (current name of child)
born on _____ , _____ , although I am listed as the father on his/her
             (date of birth)
Certificate of Live Birth.

3. Consent.

I hereby consent to having the child's name changed. I hereby join in the foregoing
Petition and waive notice of process. I acknowledge that I have the right to revoke my consent at
any time prior to when an order changing the child's name is entered. I acknowledge that I was
provided the opportunity to consult with legal counsel, if I so chose, before signing this Consent.

I SOLEMNLY AFFIRM under the penalties of perjury that the contents of the foregoing
Consent are true to the best of my knowledge, information, and belief.

_____   _____
(date)   (your signature)

                                     _____
                                     (your name - PRINTED)

                                     _____
                                     (street address)

                                     _____
                                     (city , state , zip code)

                                     _____
                                     (telephone number)

NOTE: Changing a child's name will not change an existing child support obligation.

Page 1 of 1

DR 64 - Revised 13 Feb 2001

IN THE MATTER OF: *   IN THE

_____   *   CIRCUIT COURT
(child's current name)

FOR CHANGE OF NAME TO: *   FOR

                                          *   _____

_____   *
(child's new name)

BY AND THROUGH HIS/HER   *   Civil No.:_____
MOTHER/FATHER/GUARDIAN:

_____   *
(petitioner's name)

*   *   *   *   *   *   *   *   *   *   *   *   *

NOTICE
(Minor)
(DOM REL 65)

    The above Petitioner has filed a Petition for Change of Name in which he/she seeks to change the name of a minor child from _____ to
                (The child's current legal name)
_____ . The petitioner is seeking this name change
      (name you want for the minor child)
for the child for the following reasons:

    Any person may file an objection to the Petition on or before the _____ day of

_____ , _____ . The objection must be supported by an

affidavit and served upon the Petitioner in accordance with Maryland Rule 1-321. Failure to file

an objection or affidavit within the time allowed may result in a judgment by default or the

granting of the relief sought.

_____
                    CLERK

Page 1 of 1   DR 65 - 4 February 2002

Circuit Court for_____ **Case No.**_____
City or County

Name _____ Name _____

Street Address _____ Apt. # _____   VS.   Street Address _____ Apt. # _____

City _____ State _ Zip Code _ Area Code _ Telephone   City _____ State _ Zip Code _ Area Code _ Telephone

         Plaintiff   *Defendant*

CERTIFICATE OF PUBLICATION
(DOM REL 75)

I HEREBY CERTIFY that I caused the publication of the attached notice one time in the following newspaper of general circulation: _____.
Name of Newspaper

The notice was published on _____, more than 15 days prior to the date specified in the notice for filing an objection to the Petition for Name Change.

_____   _____
Date   Signature

Attach Notice Here

Page 1 of 1

DR75 - Revised 6 May 2002

IN THE MATTER OF   *   IN THE

_____   *   CIRCUIT COURT

(your current name)   *   FOR

FOR CHANGE OF NAME TO

                 *   _____

_____

(new name)   *   Civil No.:_____

*   *   *   *   *   *   *   *   *   *   *   *   *

ORDER FOR CHANGE OF NAME

1. BASIS

The provisions of this order are based upon

[   ] **An evidentiary hearing before a [   ] Judge   [   ] Master.**

[   ] **A ruling by the court without a hearing.**

2. ORDER

UPON CONSIDERATION of the Petition to Change Name filed in this matter, it is hereby

ORDERED that the name of _____ be and the same is

changed to. _____

_____

JUDGE

Page 1 of 1   JO 12 - Revised 2 November 2000

APPENDIX 6:
SAMPLE CONSENT FORM

Civil Court of the City of New York
County of _____   Index Number _____

_____
In the Matter of the Application of

                                                          CONSENT
for Leave to Change His/Her Name To

_____

STATE OF NEW YORK, COUNTY OF _____ ss.:

_____, being duly sworn, says:

    I am (over the age of eighteen) (fourteen years of age or over) and reside at

_____

    I am (the Minor child) (the parent of the Minor child) (Spouse of the Petitioner) herein

    I have read the within Petition dated _____ _____, requesting a change

of name from _____ to _____

    I consent to such change.

                              _____
                              Signature of Affiant in the presence of the Notary

Sworn to before me this

_____ day of _____, 20____.

_____
Notary Public

CIV-GP-82C (Revised October, 2003

APPENDIX 7:
CHECKLIST OF PLACES TO CONTACT
FOLLOWING NAME CHANGE

Following is a list of some of the places you need to notify when you change your name. This is by no means an exhaustive list, and some may not apply to you, therefore, you should add to and delete from the list as your situation dictates.

1. The Social Security Administration

2. State Department of Motor Vehicles

3. Insurance agents

4. Employer

5. Banks and other financial institutions

6. Landlord or mortgage company

7. Taxing authorities

8. Utilities

9. Creditors and debtors

10. Medical providers

11. Legal representatives

12. U.S. Post Office

13. Union

14. Voter Registration Office

15. Selective Service Office

16. Friends and family

17. Department of Vital Statistics

18. U.S. Passport Office

19. Medicare/Medicaid/Public Assistance Agencies

20. Veterans Administration Office

21. U.S. Citizenship and Immigration Services

APPENDIX 8:
CHECKLIST OF DOCUMENTS TO AMEND
OR REPLACE FOLLOWING NAME CHANGE

Following is a list of some of the documents that should be replaced or amended after your name change is approved. This is by no means an exhaustive list, and some may not apply to you, therefore, you should add to and delete from the list as your situation dictates.

1. Wills (your will and wills in which you are a beneficiary)

2. Trusts

3. Powers of Attorney

4. Living Will

5. Social Security Card

6. Driver's License

7. Contracts

8. Birth Certificate

9. Credit Cards

10. Passport

11. Bank documents, e.g., checks, savings account, CDs, etc.

12. Investment documents, e.g., stocks, bonds, mutual funds, etc.

13. Real estate documents, e.g., deed, mortgage, lease, etc.

14. Health and retirement plan cards

15. Medicare/Medicaid/public assistance identification cards

16. Voter registration card

17. Car registration

17. Car registration

18. Insurance documents, e.g., house, auto and life insurance policies, etc.

19. Union, club and association membership identifications

20. Frequent flyer and other similar programs

21. Citizenship documents

APPENDIX 9:
DIRECTORY OF STATE BUREAUS OF VITAL RECORDS

STATE	ADDRESS
Alabama	Alabama Vital Records, State Department of Public Health, P.O. Box 5625, Montgomery, AL 36103-5625
Alaska	Bureau of Vital Statistics, Department of Health and Social Services, 5441 Commercial Boulevard, Juneau, AK 99801
Arizona	Office of Vital Records, P.O. Box 3887, Phoenix, AZ 85030-3887
Arkansas	Division of Vital Records, Arkansas Department of Health, 4815 West Markham Street, Little Rock, AR 72205-3867
California	Office of Vital Records, P.O. Box 997410, Sacramento, CA 95899-7410
Colorado	Vital Records Section, Department of Public Health and Environment, 4300 Cherry Creek Drive South, Denver, CO 80246-1530
Connecticut	Request must be submitted to town or city where event occurred
Delaware	Division of Public Health, P.O. Box 637, Dover, DE 19903
District of Columbia	825 North Capitol Street NE, lst Floor, Washington, DC 20002
Florida	Office of Vital Statistics, P.O. Box 210, 1217 Pearl Street, Jacksonville, FL 32231
Georgia	Vital Records, 2600 Skyland Drive, NE, Atlanta,,GA 30319-3640
Hawaii	State Department of Health, Vital Statistics Section, P.O. Box 3378, Honolulu, HI 96801

STATE	ADDRESS
Idaho	Vital Statistics, 450 West State Street, 1st Floor, P.O. Box 83720, Boise, ID 83720-0036
Illinois	Division of Vital Records, 605 West Jefferson Street, Springfield, IL 62702-5097
Indiana	Vital Records Department, 2 North Meridian Street, Indianapolis, IN 46204
Iowa	Bureau of Vital Records, 321 East 12th Street, Des Moines, IA 50319-0075
Kansas	Office of Vital Statistics State, 1000 SW Jackson Street, Topeka, Kansas 66612-2221
Kentucky	Office of Vital Statistics, 275 East Main Street, Frankfort, KY 40621-0001
Louisiana	Vital Records Registry, 325 Loyola Avenue, New Orleans, LA 70112
Maine	Office of Vital Records, 11 State House Station, Augusta, ME 04333-0011
Maryland	Division of Vital Records, 6550 Reisterstown Road, P.O. Box 68760, Baltimore, MD 21215-0020
Massachusetts	Registry of Vital Records and Statistics, 150 Mount Vernon Street, 1st Floor, Dorchester, MA 02125-3105
Michigan	Vital Records, 3423 North Martin Luther King Blvd., P.O. Box 30195, Lansing, MI 48909
Minnesota	Minnesota Department of Health, Section of Vital Statistics, 717 Delaware Street SE, P.O. Box 9441, Minneapolis, MN 55440
Mississippi	Vital Records, P.O. Box 1700, Jackson, MS 39215-1700
Missouri	Bureau of Vital Records, 930 Wildwood, P.O. Box 570, Jefferson City, MO 65102-0570
Nebraska	Vital Records, 301 Centennial Mall South, P.O. Box 95065, Lincoln, NE 68509-5065
Nevada	Office of Vital Records, Capitol Complex, 505 East King Street, Suite #102, Carson City, NV 89710
New Hampshire	Bureau of Vital Records, 6 Hazen Drive, Concord, NH 03301
New Jersey	Vital Statistics Registration, P.O. Box 370, Trenton, NJ 08625-0370
New Mexico	Vital Records, P.O. Box 26110, Santa Fe, NM 87502
New York	Vital Records Section, P.O. Box 2602, Albany, NY 12220-2602

STATE	ADDRESS
North Carolina	Vital Records, 1903 Mail Service Center, Raleigh, NC 27699-1903
North Dakota	Division of Vital Records, 600 East Boulevard Avenue, Dept.301, Bismarck, ND 58505-0200
Ohio	Bureau of Vital Statistics, 246 North High Street, 1st Floor, Columbus, OH 43216
Oklahoma	Vital Records Service, 1000 Northeast 10th Street, Oklahoma City, OK 73117
Oregon	Vital Records, P.O. Box 14050, Portland, OR 97293-0050
Pennsylvania	Division of Vital Records, 101 South Mercer Street, Room 401, P.O. Box 1528, New Castle, PA 16101
Rhode Island	Office of Vital Records, 3 Capitol Hill, Room 101, Providence, RI 02908-5097
Tennessee	Vital Records, 421 5th Avenue North, Nashville, TN 37247
Texas	Bureau of Vital Statistics, P.O. Box 12040, Austin, TX 78711-2040
Utah	Office of Vital Records, 288 North 1460 West, P.O. Box 141012, Salt Lake City, UT 84114-1012
Vermont	Department of Health, Vital Records Section, P.O. Box 70, 108 Cherry Street, Burlington, VT 05402-0070
Virginia	Office of Vital Records, P.O. Box 1000, Richmond, VA 23218-1000
Washington	Department of Health, P.O. Box 9709, Olympia, WA 98507-9709

Source: National Center for Health Statistics

APPENDIX 10:
DIRECTORY OF STATE DEPARTMENT OF MOTOR VEHICLE OFFICES

STATE	ADDRESS
Alaska	IVR Registration, 3300 B Fairbanks St., Anchorage, AK 99503
Arizona	Arizona Motor Vehicle Division, P.O. Box 2100, Mail Drop 539M, Phoenix, AZ 85001
Arkansas	Arkansas Driving Records, Room 127, P. O. Box 1272, Little Rock, AR 72203
California	California Department of Motor Vehicles, Office of Information Services, Public Operations Unit G199, P. O. Box 944247, Sacramento, CA 94244-2470
Colorado	Colorado Department of Revenue, Motor Vehicle Division, 1881 Pierce St., Lakewood, CO 80214
Connecticut	Connecticut Department of Motor Vehicles, 60 State St., Wethersfield, CT 06161-5070
Delaware	Delaware Motor Vehicles Dept., P.O. Box 698, Dover DE 19901
District of Columbia	Department of Motor Vehicles, 65 K Street NE, Washington, D.C. 20002
Florida	Bureau of Records, P.O. Box 5775, Tallahassee, FL 32314-5775
Georgia	Georgia Department of Public Safety MVR Unit, P.O. Box 1456, Atlanta, GA 30371-2303
Hawaii	Hawaii Motor Vehicle and Licensing Division, 1031 Nuuanu Avenue, Honolulu, HI 96817
Idaho	Idaho Transportation Department, Vehicle Services/Special Plates, P.O. Box 34, Boise, ID 83731-0034
Illinois	Illinois Secretary of State, 2701 S. Dirksen Parkway, Springfield, IL 62723

STATE	ADDRESS
Indiana	Indiana Bureau of Motor Vehicles, 100 N. Senate Ave., Indianapolis, IN 46204
Iowa	Iowa Office of Driver Services, 100 Euclid Ave., P.O. Box 9204, Des Moines, IA 50306-9204
Kansas	Kansas Department of Revenue, Kansas Division Of Motor Vehicles, P. O. Box 2188, Topeka, KS 66601-2188
Kentucky	Kentucky Transportation Cabinet, Division of Driver Licensing, 501 High Street, Frankfort, KY 40622
Louisiana	Office of Motor Vehicles, P.O. Box 64886, Baton Rouge, LA 70896
Maine	Bureau of Motor Vehicles, 29 State House Station, Augusta, ME 04333-0029
Maryland	Maryland Department of Transportation, Motor Vehicle Administration, 6601 Ritchie Highway, N.E., Glen Burnie, MD 21062
Massachusetts	Massachusetts Registry of Motor Vehicles Driver Control Unit, Attn: Court Records, P.O. Box 199150, Boston, MA 02119-9150
Michigan	Michigan Department of State, Record Lookup Unit, 7064 Crowner Drive, Lansing, MI 48918-1540
Minnesota	Minnesota Department of Public Safety, Driver and Vehicle Services, 445 Minnesota Street, St. Paul, MN 55101
Mississippi	Mississippi Department of Public Safety, Driver Records Branch, P. O. Box 958, Jackson, MS 39205
Missouri	Drivers License Bureau, P.O. Box 200, Jefferson City, MO 65105
Montana	Records and Driver Control Bureau, Second Floor, Scott Hart Building, P.O. Box 201430, 303 N. Roberts, Helena, MT 59620-1430
Nebraska	Nebraska Department of Motor Vehicles, State Office Building, 301 Centennial Mall South, Lincoln, NE 68509
Nevada	Nevada Department of Motor Vehicles and Public Safety, Drivers License Division, 555 Wright Way, Carson City, NV 89711
New Hampshire	James H. Hayes Building, 10 Hazen Drive, Concord, NH 03305-0002
New Jersey	New Jersey Motor Vehicle Services, P.O. Box 160, 225 East State St., Trenton, NJ 08666
New Mexico	New Mexico Motor Vehicle Division, P.O. Box 1028, Joseph Montoya Bldg., Santa Fe, NM 87504
New York	New York State Department of Motor Vehicles, 6 Empire State Plaza, Room 430, Albany, NY 12228

STATE	ADDRESS
North Carolina	North Carolina DMV, Driver License Section, 1100 New Bern Ave., Raleigh, NC 27697
North Dakota	North Dakota Drivers License, Traffic Safety, 608 E Boulevard Ave, Bismarck, ND 58505-0700
Ohio	Ohio Bureau of Motor Vehicles, Attn: MVOSDM, P.O. Box 16520, Columbus, OH 43266-0020
Oklahoma	Oklahoma Department of Public Safety, 3600 North Martin Luther King Blvd., Oklahoma City, OK 73111
Oregon	Oregon DMV Headquarters, Attn: Record Services, 1905 Lana Ave. NE, Salem, OR, 97314
Pennsylvania	Pennsylvania Department of Transportation, Bureau of Driver Licensing, Driver Record Services, P.O. Box 68695, Harrisburg, PA 17106-8695
Rhode Island	Division of Motor Vehicles, 286 Main Street, Pawtucket, RI 02860
South Carolina	Division of Motor Vehicles, P.O. Box 1498, Columbia, SC 29216
South Dakota	South Dakota Department of Commerce and Regulation, Drivers License, 118 West Capitol, Pierre, SD 57501
Tennessee	Tennessee Department of Safety, 1150 Foster Avenue, Nashville, TN 37249
Texas	Texas Department of Transportation, Vehicle Titles and Registration Division, Austin, TX 78779-0001
Utah	Administrative Office, 210 North 1950 West, Salt Lake City, UT 84134
Vermont	Vermont Agency of Transportation, Department Of Motor Vehicles, 120 State Street, Montpelier, VT 05603-0001
Virginia	Virginia Department of Motor Vehicles, P.O. Box 27412, Richmond, VA 23269
Washington	Department of Licensing, P.O. Box 9030, Olympia, WA 98507-9030
West Virginia	West Virginia Division of Motor Vehicles, 1800 Kanawha Boulevard East, Charleston, WV 25317
Wisconsin	Wisconsin Department of Transportation, P.O. Box 7995, 4802 Sheboygan Avenue, Madison, WI 53707-7995
Wyoming	Wyoming Department of Transportation/Driver Services, P.O. Box 1708, Cheyenne, WY 82003-1708

APPENDIX 11:
APPLICATION FOR SOCIAL SECURITY CARD (FORM SS-5)

SOCIAL SECURITY ADMINISTRATION
Application for a Social Security Card

Applying for a Social Security Card is easy <u>AND</u> it is free!

USE THIS APPLICATION TO APPLY FOR:

• An **original** Social Security card
• A **duplicate** Social Security card (same name and number)
• A **corrected** Social Security card (name change and same number)
• A **change of information** on your record other than your name (no card needed)

IMPORTANT: You MUST provide the required evidence or we cannot process the application. Follow the instructions below to provide the information and evidence we need.

STEP 1   Read pages 1 through 3 which explain how to complete the application and what evidence we need.
STEP 2   Complete and sign the application using BLUE or BLACK ink. Do not use pencil or other colors of ink. Please print legibly.
STEP 3   Submit the completed and signed application with all required evidence to any Social Security office.

HOW TO COMPLETE THIS APPLICATION

Most items on the form are self-explanatory. Those that need explanation are discussed below. The numbers match the numbered items on the form. If you are completing this form for someone else, please complete the items as they apply to that person.

2.   Show the address where you can receive your card 10 to 14 days from now.

3.   If you check "Legal Alien **Not** Allowed to Work," you need to provide a document from the government agency requiring your Social Security number that explains why you need a number and that you meet all of the requirements for the benefit or service except for the number. A State or local agency requirement must conform with Federal law.

     If you check "Other," you need to provide proof you are entitled to a federally-funded benefit for which a Social Security number is required as a condition for you to receive payment.

5.   Providing race/ethnic information is voluntary. However, if you do give us this information, it helps us prepare statistical reports on how Social Security programs affect people. We do not reveal the identities of individuals.

6.   Show the month, day and full (4 digit) year of birth, for example, "1998" for year of birth.

8.B.   Show the mother's Social Security number only if you are applying for an original Social Security card for a child under age 18. You may leave this item blank if the mother does not have a number or you do not know the mother's number. We will still be able to assign a number to the child.

9.B.   Show the father's Social Security number only if you are applying for an original Social Security card for a child under age 18. You may leave this item blank if the father does not have a number or you do not know the father's number. We will still be able to assign a number to the child.

Form **SS-5** (10-2003) EF (10-2003) Destroy Prior Editions   Page 1

APPLICATION FOR SOCIAL SECURITY CARD (FORM SS-5)

13. If the date of birth you show in item 6 is different from the date of birth you used on a prior application for a Social Security card, show the date of birth you used on the prior application and submit evidence of age to support the date of birth in item 6.

16. You **must** sign the application yourself if you are age 18 or older and are physically and mentally capable. If you are under age 18, you may also sign the application if you are physically and mentally capable. If you cannot sign your name, you should sign with an "X" mark and have two people sign as witnesses in the space beside the mark. If you are physically or mentally incapable of signing the application, generally a parent, close relative, or legal guardian may sign the application. Call us if you need clarification about who can sign.

ABOUT YOUR DOCUMENTS

- We need **ORIGINAL** documents or **copies certified by the custodian of the record.** We will return your documents after we have seen them.

- **We cannot accept photocopies or notarized copies of documents.**

- If your documents do not meet this requirement, we cannot process your application.

DOCUMENTS WE NEED

To apply for an **ORIGINAL CARD** (you have NEVER been assigned a Social Security number before), we need at least 2 documents as proof of:

- **Age,**
- **Identity, and**
- **U.S. citizenship or lawful alien status.**

To apply for a **DUPLICATE CARD** (same number, same name), we need proof of **identity**.

To apply for a **CORRECTED CARD** (same number, different name), we need proof of **identity**. We need one or more documents which identify you by the OLD NAME on our records and your NEW NAME. Examples include: a marriage certificate, divorce decree, or a court order that changes your name. Or we can accept two identity documents - one in your old name and one in your new name. (See IDENTITY, for examples of identity documents.)

IMPORTANT: If you are applying for a duplicate or corrected card and were **born outside the U.S.**, we also need proof of U.S. citizenship or lawful alien status. (See U.S. CITIZENSHIP or ALIEN STATUS for examples of documents you can submit.)

AGE: We prefer to see your birth certificate. However, we can accept another document that shows your age. Some of the other documents we can accept are:

- Hospital record of your birth (created at the time of your birth)
- Religious record showing your age made before you were 3 months old
- Passport
- Adoption record (the adoption record must indicate that the birth data was taken from the original birth certificate)

Call us for advice if you cannot obtain one of these documents.

Form **SS-5** (10-2003) EF (10-2003)   Page 2

IDENTITY: We must see a document in the name you want shown on the card. The identity document must be of recent issuance so that we can determine your continued existence. We prefer to see a document with a photograph. However, we can generally accept a non-photo identity document if it has enough information to identify you (e.g., your name, as well as age, date of birth or parents' names). **WE CANNOT ACCEPT A BIRTH CERTIFICATE, HOSPITAL SOUVENIR BIRTH CERTIFICATE, SOCIAL SECURITY CARD OR CARD STUB, OR SOCIAL SECURITY RECORD** as evidence of identity. Some documents we can accept are:

- Driver's license
- Employee ID card
- Passport
- Marriage or divorce record
- Adoption record (only if not being used to establish age)
- Health insurance card (not a Medicare card)
- Military record
- Life insurance policy
- School ID card

As evidence of identity for infants and young children, we can accept :

- Doctor, clinic, hospital record
- Daycare center, school record
- Religious record (e.g., baptismal record)

IMPORTANT: If you are **applying for a card on behalf of someone else,** you must provide evidence that establishes your authority to sign the application on behalf of the person to whom the card will be issued. In addition, we must see proof of identity for both you and the person to whom the card will be issued.

U. S. CITIZENSHIP: We can accept most documents that show you were born in the U.S. If you are a U.S. citizen born outside the U.S., show us a U.S. consular report of birth, a U.S. passport, a Certificate of Citizenship, or a Certificate of Naturalization.

ALIEN STATUS: We need to see an unexpired document issued to you by the Department of Homeland Security (DHS) showing your immigration status, such as Form I-551, I-94, I-688B, or I-766. We CANNOT accept a receipt showing you applied for the document. If you are not authorized to work in the U.S., we can issue you a Social Security card if you are lawfully here and need the number for a valid nonwork reason. (See HOW TO COMPLETE THIS APPLICATION, Item 3.) Your card will be marked to show you cannot work. If you do work, we will notify DHS.

To **CHANGE INFORMATION** on your record other than your name, we need proof of:

- **Identity,** and
- **Another document which supports the change** (for example, a birth certificate to change your date and/or place of birth or parents' names).

HOW TO SUBMIT THIS APPLICATION

In most cases, you can mail this application with your evidence documents to any Social Security office. We will return your documents to you. If you do not want to mail your original documents, take them with this application to the nearest Social Security office.

EXCEPTION: If you are age 12 or older and have never been assigned a number before, you must apply in person.

If you have any questions about this form, or about the documents we need, please contact any Social Security office. A telephone call will help you make sure you have everything you need to apply for a card or change information on your record. You can find your nearest office in your local phone directory or on our website at www.socialsecurity.gov.

Form **SS-5** (10-2003) EF (10-2003)   Page 3

THE PAPERWORK/PRIVACY ACT AND YOUR APPLICATION

The Privacy Act of 1974 requires us to give each person the following notice when applying for a Social Security number.

Sections 205(c) and 702 of the Social Security Act allow us to collect the facts we ask for on this form.

We use the facts you provide on this form to assign you a Social Security number and to issue you a Social Security card. You do not have to give us these facts, however, without them we cannot issue you a Social Security number or a card. Without a number, you may not be able to get a job and could lose Social Security benefits in the future.

The Social Security number is also used by the Internal Revenue Service for tax administration purposes as an identifier in processing tax returns of persons who have income which is reported to the Internal Revenue Service and by persons who are claimed as dependents on someone's Federal income tax return.

We may disclose information as necessary to administer Social Security programs, including to appropriate law enforcement agencies to investigate alleged violations of Social Security law; to other government agencies for administering entitlement, health, and welfare programs such as Medicaid, Medicare, veterans benefits, military pension, and civil service annuities, black lung, housing, student loans, railroad retirement benefits, and food stamps; to the Internal Revenue Service for Federal tax administration; and to employers and former employers to properly prepare wage reports. We may also disclose information as required by Federal law, for example, to the Department of Homeland Security, to identify and locate aliens in the U.S.; to the Selective Service System for draft registration; and to the Department of Health and Human Services for child support enforcement purposes. We may verify Social Security numbers for State motor vehicle agencies that use the number in issuing drivers licenses, as authorized by the Social Security Act. Finally, we may disclose information to your Congressional representative if they request information to answer questions you ask him or her.

We may use the information you give us when we match records by computer. Matching programs compare our records with those of other Federal, State, or local government agencies to determine whether a person qualifies for benefits paid by the Federal government. The law allows us to do this even if you do not agree to it.

Explanations about these and other reasons why information you provide us may be used or given out are available in Social Security offices. If you want to learn more about this, contact any Social Security office.

This information collection meets the requirements of 44 U.S.C. §3507, as amended by Section 2 of the Paperwork Reduction Act of 1995. You do not need to answer these questions unless we display a valid Office of Management and Budget control number. We estimate that it will take about 8.5 to 9 minutes to read the instructions, gather the facts, and answer the questions. **SEND THE COMPLETED FORM TO YOUR LOCAL SOCIAL SECURITY OFFICE. The office is listed under U. S. Government agencies in your telephone directory or you may call Social Security at 1-800-772-1213.** *You may send comments on our time estimate above to: SSA, 1338 Annex Building, Baltimore, MD 21235-0001.* **Send only comments relating to our time estimate to this address, not the completed form.**

Form **SS-5** (10-2003) EF (10-2003)   Page 4

SOCIAL SECURITY ADMINISTRATION
Application for a Social Security Card

Form Approved
OMB No. 0960-0066

		First	Full Middle Name	Last
	NAME ⟶ TO BE SHOWN ON CARD			
1	FULL NAME AT BIRTH IF OTHER THAN ABOVE	First	Full Middle Name	Last
	OTHER NAMES USED			

2	MAILING ADDRESS Do Not Abbreviate	Street Address, Apt. No., PO Box, Rural Route No.		
		City	State	Zip Code

3 CITIZENSHIP ⟶ (Check One)
☐ U.S. Citizen   ☐ Legal Alien Allowed To Work   ☐ Legal Alien **Not** Allowed To Work (See Instructions On Page 1)   ☐ Other (See Instructions On Page 1)

4 SEX ⟶
☐ Male   ☐ Female

5 RACE/ETHNIC DESCRIPTION (Check One Only - Voluntary)
☐ Asian, Asian-American or Pacific Islander   ☐ Hispanic   ☐ Black (Not Hispanic)   ☐ North American Indian or Alaskan Native   ☐ White (Not Hispanic)

6 DATE OF BIRTH   Month, Day, Year

7 PLACE OF BIRTH (Do Not Abbreviate)   City   State or Foreign Country   FCI

Office Use Only

8	A. MOTHER'S MAIDEN NAME ⟶	First	Full Middle Name	Last Name At Her Birth
	B. MOTHER'S SOCIAL SECURITY NUMBER ⟶	☐☐☐ – ☐☐ – ☐☐☐☐		

9	A. FATHER'S NAME ⟶	First	Full Middle Name	Last
	B. FATHER'S SOCIAL SECURITY NUMBER ⟶	☐☐☐ – ☐☐ – ☐☐☐☐		

10 Has the applicant or anyone acting on his/her behalf ever filed for or received a Social Security number card before?
☐ Yes (If "yes", answer questions 11-13.)   ☐ No (If "no", go on to question 14.)   ☐ Don't Know (If "don't know", go on to question 14.)

11 Enter the Social Security number previously assigned to the person listed in item 1. ⟶   ☐☐☐ – ☐☐ – ☐☐☐☐

12 Enter the name shown on the most recent Social Security card issued for the person listed in item 1. ⟶   First   Middle Name   Last

13 Enter any different date of birth if used on an earlier application for a card. ⟶   Month, Day, Year

14 TODAY'S DATE   Month, Day, Year

15 DAYTIME PHONE NUMBER   ( )   Area Code   Number

I declare under penalty of perjury that I have examined all the information on this form, and on any accompanying statements or forms, and it is true and correct to the best of my knowledge.

16 YOUR SIGNATURE ▶

17 YOUR RELATIONSHIP TO THE PERSON IN ITEM 1 IS:
☐ Self   ☐ Natural Or Adoptive Parent   ☐ Legal Guardian   ☐ Other (Specify)

DO NOT WRITE BELOW THIS LINE (FOR SSA USE ONLY)

NPN			DOC	NTI	CAN		ITV
PBC	EVI	EVA	EVC	PRA	NWR	DNR	UNIT
EVIDENCE SUBMITTED					SIGNATURE AND TITLE OF EMPLOYEE(S) REVIEWING EVIDENCE AND/OR CONDUCTING INTERVIEW		
							DATE
					DCL		DATE

Form **SS-5** (10-2003) EF (10-2003) Destroy Prior Editions   Page 5

APPENDIX 12
PASSPORT AMENDMENT/VALIDATION
APPLICATION (FORM DS-19)

U.S. Department of State

U.S. PASSPORT AMENDMENT/VALIDATION APPLICATION
Type or print in ink in white areas only. For more information, see back of form.

IDENTIFYING INFORMATION
CURRENT NAME

FIRST | MIDDLE

LAST

SOCIAL SECURITY NUMBER

MAILING ADDRESS

STREET

HOME PHONE (with Area Code)

CITY, STATE,
& ZIP CODE

IN CARE OF

BUSINESS PHONE (with Area Code)

SEX   PLACE OF BIRTH   DATE OF BIRTH   DEPARTURE DATE, If Any

☐ ☐
Male Female   City, State or Province, Country   *(mm-dd-yyyy)*   *(mm-dd-yyyy)*

U.S. PASSPORT NUMBER   DATE YOUR PASSPORT WAS ISSUED   PLACE YOUR PASSPORT WAS ISSUED

(mm-dd-yyyy)

PERMANENT ADDRESS (Street, City, State, Zip Code)   E-MAIL ADDRESS

NAME CHANGE *(Submit original or certified document)*

NAME CURRENTLY IN PASSPORT   CHANGE NAME TO READ AS FOLLOWS:

● **NAME CHANGED BY MARRIAGE**
DATE OF MARRIAGE   SPOUSE'S NAME IN FULL

(mm-dd-yyyy)

● **NAME CHANGED BY COURT ORDER**
NAME OF COURT   LOCATION (City, State)   DATE

(mm-dd-yyyy)

● **NAME CHANGED BY OTHER METHOD (Specify)**

OTHER PASSPORT REQUESTS: *(Check appropriate box and specify, where necessary)*

☐ ADD VISA PAGES   ☐ CORRECT DESCRIPTIVE DATA (Specify)

☐ EXTEND PASSPORT VALIDITY   ☐ OTHER (Specify)

OATH AND SIGNATURE I have not, since acquiring United States citizenship, performed any of the acts listed under "Acts or Conditions" on this application form (unless an explanatory statement is attached). I solemnly swear (or affirm) that the statements made on this application are true.

FOR PASSPORT SERVICES USE ONLY

Date *(mm-dd-yyyy)*   Signature of Applicant

☐ Evidence   ☐ Extend To
☐ Name Change   ☐ Endorsement No.   Examiner's Name
☐ Add Visa Pages   ☐ Limit To
☐ Rewrite   ☐ Void Limitation on Page
☐ Other   Office.   Date *(mm-dd-yyyy)*

DS-19
04-2003   OMB No. 1405-0007 Expires: 12/31/2005 Estimated Burden 5 Minutes (See Page 2)   Page 1 of 2

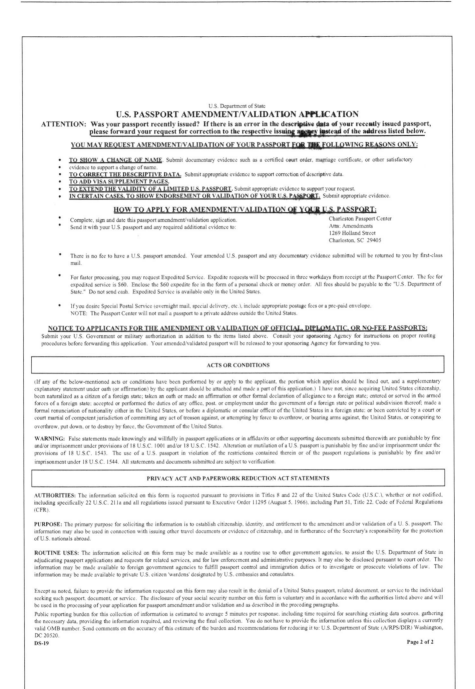

U.S. Department of State

U.S. PASSPORT AMENDMENT/VALIDATION APPLICATION

ATTENTION: Was your passport recently issued? If there is an error in the descriptive data of your recently issued passport, please forward your request for correction to the respective issuing agency instead of the address listed below.

YOU MAY REQUEST AMENDMENT/VALIDATION OF YOUR PASSPORT FOR THE FOLLOWING REASONS ONLY:

- **TO SHOW A CHANGE OF NAME.** Submit documentary evidence such as a certified court order, marriage certificate, or other satisfactory evidence to support a change of name.
- **TO CORRECT THE DESCRIPTIVE DATA.** Submit appropriate evidence to support correction of descriptive data.
- **TO ADD VISA SUPPLEMENT PAGES.**
- **TO EXTEND THE VALIDITY OF A LIMITED U.S. PASSPORT.** Submit appropriate evidence to support your request.
- **IN CERTAIN CASES, TO SHOW ENDORSEMENT OR VALIDATION OF YOUR U.S. PASSPORT.** Submit appropriate evidence.

HOW TO APPLY FOR AMENDMENT/VALIDATION OF YOUR U.S. PASSPORT:

- Complete, sign and date this passport amendment/validation application.
- Send it with your U.S. passport and any required additional evidence to:

  Charleston Passport Center
  Attn: Amendments
  1269 Holland Street
  Charleston, SC 29405

- There is no fee to have a U.S. passport amended. Your amended U.S. passport and any documentary evidence submitted will be returned to you by first-class mail.

- For faster processing, you may request Expedited Service. Expedite requests will be processed in three workdays from receipt at the Passport Center. The fee for expedited service is $60. Enclose the $60 expedite fee in the form of a personal check or money order. All fees should be payable to the "U.S. Department of State." Do not send cash. Expedited Service is available only in the United States.

- If you desire Special Postal Service (overnight mail, special delivery, etc.), include appropriate postage fees or a pre-paid envelope. NOTE: The Passport Center will not mail a passport to a private address outside the United States.

NOTICE TO APPLICANTS FOR THE AMENDMENT OR VALIDATION OF OFFICIAL, DIPLOMATIC, OR NO-FEE PASSPORTS:

Submit your U.S. Government or military authorization in addition to the items listed above. Consult your sponsoring Agency for instructions on proper routing procedures before forwarding this application. Your amended/validated passport will be released to your sponsoring Agency for forwarding to you.

ACTS OR CONDITIONS

(If any of the below-mentioned acts or conditions have been performed by or apply to the applicant, the portion which applies should be lined out, and a supplementary explanatory statement under oath (or affirmation) by the applicant should be attached and made a part of this application.) I have not, since acquiring United States citizenship, been naturalized as a citizen of a foreign state; taken an oath or made an affirmation or other formal declaration of allegiance to a foreign state; entered or served in the armed forces of a foreign state; accepted or performed the duties of any office, post, or employment under the government of a foreign state or political subdivision thereof; made a formal renunciation of nationality either in the United States, or before a diplomatic or consular officer of the United States in a foreign state; or been convicted by a court or court martial of competent jurisdiction of committing any act of treason against, or attempting by force to overthrow, or bearing arms against, the United States, or conspiring to overthrow, put down, or to destroy by force, the Government of the United States.

WARNING: False statements made knowingly and willfully in passport applications or in affidavits or other supporting documents submitted therewith are punishable by fine and/or imprisonment under provisions of 18 U.S.C. 1001 and/or 18 U.S.C. 1542. Alteration or mutilation of a U.S. passport is punishable by fine and/or imprisonment under the provisions of 18 U.S.C. 1543. The use of a U.S. passport in violation of the restrictions contained therein or of the passport regulations is punishable by fine and/or imprisonment under 18 U.S.C. 1544. All statements and documents submitted are subject to verification.

PRIVACY ACT AND PAPERWORK REDUCTION ACT STATEMENTS

AUTHORITIES: The information solicited on this form is requested pursuant to provisions in Titles 8 and 22 of the United States Code (U.S.C.), whether or not codified, including specifically 22 U.S.C. 211a and all regulations issued pursuant to Executive Order 11295 (August 5, 1966), including Part 51, Title 22, Code of Federal Regulations (CFR).

PURPOSE: The primary purpose for soliciting the information is to establish citizenship, identity, and entitlement to the amendment and/or validation of a U. S. passport. The information may also be used in connection with issuing other travel documents or evidence of citizenship, and in furtherance of the Secretary's responsibility for the protection of U.S. nationals abroad.

ROUTINE USES: The information solicited on this form may be made available as a routine use to other government agencies, to assist the U.S. Department of State in adjudicating passport applications and requests for related services, and for law enforcement and administrative purposes. It may also be disclosed pursuant to court order. The information may be made available to foreign government agencies to fulfill passport control and immigration duties or to investigate or prosecute violations of law. The information may be made available to private U.S. citizen 'wardens' designated by U.S. embassies and consulates.

Except as noted, failure to provide the information requested on this form may also result in the denial of a United States passport, related document, or service to the individual seeking such passport, document, or service. The disclosure of your social security number on this form is voluntary and in accordance with the authorities listed above and will be used in the processing of your application for passport amendment and/or validation and as described in the preceding paragraphs.

Public reporting burden for this collection of information is estimated to average 5 minutes per response, including time required for searching existing data sources, gathering the necessary data, providing the information required, and reviewing the final collection. You do not have to provide the information unless this collection displays a currently valid OMB number. Send comments on the accuracy of this estimate of the burden and recommendations for reducing it to: U.S. Department of State (A/RPS/DIR) Washington, DC 20520.

DS-19   Page 2 of 2

APPENDIX 13:
DIRECTORY OF PASSPORT AGENCIES

REGION	ADDRESS	TELEPHONE	HOURS	SERVICES PROVIDED
Boston Passport Agency	Thomas P. O'Neill Federal Building 10 Causeway Street Suite 247 Boston, MA 02222-1094	(877) 487-2778	8:30 a.m. - 4:30 p.m. local time, M-F excluding Federal holidays	serves customers traveling within 14 days or those who need foreign visas for travel. An appointment is required.
Chicago Passport Agency	Kluczynski Federal Building 230 S. Dearborn Street 18th Floor, Chicago, IL 60604-1564	(312) 341-6020	9:00 a.m. - 4:00 p.m. local time, M-F excluding Federal holidays	serves customers who are traveling within 14 days or who need foreign visas for travel. An appointment is required.

REGION	ADDRESS	TELEPHONE	HOURS	SERVICES PROVIDED
Connecticut Passport Agency	50 Washington Street Norwalk, CT 06854	(203) 299-5443	9:00 a.m. - 4:00 p.m. local time, M-F excluding Federal holidays	serves customers who are traveling within 14 days or who need foreign visas for travel. An appointment is required.
Honolulu Passport Agency	Prince Kuhio Federal Building 300 Ala Moana Blvd. Suite 1-330 Honolulu, HI 96850	(808) 522-8283	8:30 a.m. - 3:30 p.m. local time, M-F excluding Federal holidays	serves customers who are traveling within 14 days or who need foreign visas for travel. An appointment is required.
Houston Passport Agency	Mickey Leland Federal Building, 1919 Smith Street Suite 1400 Houston, TX 77002-8049	(713) 751-0294	8:30 a.m. - 3:30 p.m. local time, M-F excluding Federal holidays	serves customers who are traveling within 14 days or who need foreign visas for travel. An appointment is required.
Los Angeles Passport Agency	Federal Building, 11000 Wilshire Blvd.., Suite 1000 Los Angeles, CA 90024-3615	(310) 575-5700	8:00 a.m. - 3:00 p.m. local time, M-F excluding Federal holidays	serves customers who are traveling within 14 days or who need foreign visas for travel. An appointment is required.

REGION	ADDRESS	TELEPHONE	HOURS	SERVICES PROVIDED
Miami Passport Agency	Claude Pepper Federal Office Building, 51 SW First Avenue 3rd Floor, Miami, FL 33130-1680	(305) 539-3600	8:30 a.m. - 3:30 p.m. local time, M-F excluding Federal holidays	serves customers who are traveling within 14 days or who need foreign visas for travel. An appointment is required.
New Orleans Passport Agency	One Canal Place 365 Canal Street, Suite 1300 New Orleans, LA 70130-6508	(504) 412-2600	8:30 a.m. - 3:30 p.m. local time, M-F excluding Federal holidays	serves customers who are traveling within 14 days or who need foreign visas for travel. An appointment is required.
New York	376 Hudson Street New York, NY 10014	(212) 206-3500	7:30 a.m. - 3:00 p.m. local time, M-F excluding Federal holidays	serves customers who are traveling within 14 days or who need foreign visas for travel. An appointment is required.
Philadelphia Passport Agency	U.S. Custom House 200 Chestnut Street, Room 103 Philadelphia, PA 19106-2970	(215) 418-5937	9:00 a.m. - 4:00 p.m., local time, M-F excluding Federal holidays	serves customers who are traveling within 14 days or who need foreign visas for travel. An appointment is required.

REGION	ADDRESS	TELEPHONE	HOURS	SERVICES PROVIDED
San Francisco Passport Agency	95 Hawthorne Street 5th Floor San Francisco, CA 94105-3901	(415) 538-2700	8:00 a.m. - 3:00 p.m. local time, M-F excluding Federal holidays	serves customers who are traveling within 14 days or who need foreign visas for travel. An appointment is required.
Seattle Passport Agency	Henry Jackson Federal Building, 915 Second Avenue, Suite 992 Seattle, WA 98174-1091	(206) 808-5700	8:00 a.m. - 3:00 p.m. local time, M-F excluding Federal holidays	serves customers who are traveling within 14 days or who need foreign visas for travel. An appointment is required.
Washington D.C. Passport Agency	1111 19th Street N.W. First Floor, Sidewalk Level Washington, D.C. 20036	(202) 647-0518	8:00 a.m. - 3:00 p.m. local time, M-F excluding Federal holidays	serves customers who are traveling within 14 days or who need foreign visas for travel. An appointment is required.
Special Issuance Agency	1111 19th Street N.W. Suite 200 Washington, D.C. 20036	none listed	8:15 a.m. - 4:30 p.m. local time, M-F excluding Federal holidays	process applications for Diplomatic, Official, and No-Fee passports through two Passport Centers listed below.
Charleston Passport Center	1269 Holland Street, Charleston, SC 29405	none listed	8:00 a.m. - 4:00 p.m. local time, M-F excluding Federal holidays	Center is not open to the public.
National Passport Center	31 Rochester Avenue Portsmouth, NH 03801-290	none listed	9:00 a.m. - 4:00 p.m., M-F excluding Federal holidays	Center is not open to the public.

APPENDIX 14:
SAMPLE NAME CHANGE NOTIFICATION LETTER

Date

Name of Company
Street Address
City, State, Zip Code

RE: [Account #/Identification #/Membership #]

Dear Sir/Madam:

Please be advised that I have legally changed my name and I am hereby requesting that you amend my records accordingly, effective immediately, as follows:

The current name in your records is Mary Jones.

My new legal name is Mary Smith. I have attached [court order, marriage license, etc.] as evidence of the name change.

[If applicable] Please send me replacement [identification cards, credit cards, etc.] reflecting my new name as soon as possible.

Please send all future correspondence to me in care of my new legal name.

If you have any questions or need further information, please contact me. Thank you for your cooperation.

[Signature]

Printed Name

GLOSSARY

Acknowledgement—A formal declaration of one's signature before a notary public.

Adjudication—The determination of a controversy and pronouncement of judgment.

Adjudicatory Hearing—The process by which it is determined whether the allegations in a complaint can be proven and, if so, whether they fall within the jurisdictional categories of the juvenile court.

Adoption—Legal process pursuant to state statute in which a child's legal rights and duties toward his natural parent(s) are terminated, and similar rights and duties toward his adoptive parents are substituted.

Affiant—One who swears to an affidavit, also known as a deponent.

Affidavit—A sworn or affirmed statement made in writing and signed; if sworn, it is notarized.

Affinity—Related by marriage; family relation from one's spouse's family.

Affidavit of Service—An affidavit intended to certify the service of a writ, notice, or other document.

Affirm—An act of declaring something to be true under the penalty of perjury by a person who conscientiously declines to take an oath for religious or other pertinent reasons.

Affirmation—A solemn and formal declaration under penalties of perjury that a statement is true, without an oath.

Alien—A person who is not a citizen or national of the United States.

Amend—To make an addition to, or a subtraction from, an already existing document.

Bankruptcy—The legal process governed by federal law designed to assist the debtor in a new financial start while insuring fairness among creditors.

Beneficiary—A person who is designated to receive property upon the death of another, such as the beneficiary of a life insurance policy, who receives the proceeds upon the death of the insured.

Capacity—Capacity is the legal qualification concerning the ability of one to understand the nature and effects of one's acts.

Certified Copy—Copy of a document signed and certified as a true copy of an original by the Clerk of the Court or other authorized persons.

Child Custody—The care, control and maintenance of a child which may be awarded by a court to one of the parents of the child.

Child Support—The legal obligation of parents to contribute to the economic maintenance of their children.

Child Welfare—A generic term which embraces the totality of measures necessary for a child's well being; physical, moral and mental.

Codicil—A document modifying an existing will which, in order to be valid, must be formally drafted and witnessed according to statutory requirements.

Cohabitation—The mutual assumption of those marital rights, duties and obligations which are usually manifested by married people.

Consanguinity—Related by blood.

Contract—A contract is an agreement between two or more persons which creates an obligation to do or not to do a particular thing.

Credit—Credit is that which is extended to the buyer or borrower on the seller or lender's belief that that which is given will be repaid.

Credit Report—A credit report refers to the document from a credit reporting agency setting forth a credit rating and pertinent financial data concerning a person or a company, which is used in evaluating the applicant's financial stability.

Decree—A decision or order of the court.

Deed—A legal instrument conveying title to real property.

Dissolution of Marriage—The effect of a judgment of dissolution of marriage is to restore the parties to the state of unmarried persons.

Divorce—The legal separation of a husband and wife, effected by the judgment or decree of a court.

Durable Power of Attorney—Also known as a "health care proxy," refers to a document naming a person to make a medical decisions in the event that the individual becomes unable to make those decisions himself or herself.

Emancipated Minor—A person who, although under the age of legal adulthood, is given by state law certain rights of an adult.

Emancipation—The surrender of care, custody and earnings of a child, as well as renunciation of parental duties.

Fraud—A false representation of a matter of fact, whether by words or by conduct, by false or misleading allegations, or by concealment of that which should have been disclosed, which deceives and is intended to deceive another, and thereby causes injury to that person.

Hearing—A proceeding to determine an issue of fact based on the evidence presented.

Heir—One who inherits property.

Infancy—The period prior to reaching the legal age of majority.

Inherit—To take as an heir at law by descent rather than by will.

Inheritance—Property inherited by heirs according to the laws of descent and distribution.

Judge—The individual who presides over a court, and whose function it is to determine controversies.

Jurisdiction—The geographical, subject matter, and monetary limitations of a court to hear and determine a case.

Living Trust—A trust which is operated during the life of the creator of the trust.

Living Will—A declaration that states an individual's wishes concerning the use of extraordinary life support systems.

Medicare—The program governed by the Social Security Administration to provide medical and hospital coverage to the aged or disabled.

Minor—A person who has not yet reached the age of legal competence, which is designated as 18 in most states.

Notice of Petition—Written notice of a petitioner that a hearing will be held in a court to determine the relief requested in an annexed petition.

Oath—A sworn declaration of the truth under penalty of perjury.

Objection—The process by which it is asserted that a particular question, or piece of evidence, is improper, and it is requested that the court rule upon the objectionable matter.

Order—an oral or written direction of a court or judge.

Paralegal—An individual usually employed by a law office to perform various tasks associated with the practice of law, but one who is not licensed to practice law.

Party—Person having a direct interest in a legal matter, transaction or proceeding.

Paternity—The relationship of fatherhood.

Petition—A formal written request to a court which initiates a special proceeding.

Petitioner—In a special proceeding, one who commences a formal written application, requesting some action or relief, addressed to a court for determination.

Pro Se—Literally means for oneself; refers to a party who acts as his/her own attorney without representation.

Will—A legal document which a person executes setting forth their wishes as to the distribution of their property upon death.

BIBLIOGRAPHY AND ADDITIONAL RESOURCES

Black's Law Dictionary, Fifth Edition. St. Paul, MN: West Publishing Company, 1979.

Kibitz.com (Date Visited: March 2005)<http://www.kitbiz.com/>.

Namechangelaw.com (Date Visited: March 2005) <http://www.name changelaw.com/>.

Federal Election Committee, National Voter Registration System (Date Visited: March 2005) <http://www.fec.gov/pages/electpg.htm/>.

Nolo Press (Date Visited: March 2005) <http://www.nolopress.com/>.

Selective Service System (Date Visited: March 2005) <http://www.sss.gov/>.

U.S. Social Security Administration (Date Visited: March 2005) <http://www.ssa.gov/>.

U.S. Department of State Bureau of Consular Affairs (Date Visited: March 2005) <http://www.travel.state.gov/>.

U.S. Legal Forms (Date Visited: March 2005) <http://www.uslegal forms.com/>.